W9-AEK-570

WITHDRAWN

The Logan Bindery, 502 N. Prior Ave., St. Paul, Minn.

MARY GOES FIRST

VOLUME V

The Drama League Series of Plays

MARY GOES FIRST

A Comedy in Three Acts and an Epilogue

BY
HENRY ARTHUR JONES 1851-

Thus it appears that the Honours and Dignities adjudged by the State, serve often but to varnish the Stratagems and Pretences whereby they have been obtained; and the Claim to Precedency is shewn to be the Claim of those who have no other Claim to our Admiration and Esteem. —FETTLEWORTH'S *Credentials of Merit* (1764), Chapter on Titles.

WITH AN INTRODUCTION BY
CLAYTON HAMILTON

GARDEN CITY   NEW YORK
DOUBLEDAY, PAGE & COMPANY
1915

N. D. S. U. LIBRARY
FARGO N. D.

822
J7
cop

Copyright, 1913, by
HENRY A. JONES

Copyright, 1914, by
DOUBLEDAY PAGE & COMPANY

In its present form this play is dedicated to the reading public only, and no performances of it may be given. Any piracy or infringement will be prosecuted in accordance with the penalties provided by the United States Statutes:—

Sec. 4966. — Any person publicly performing or representing any dramatic or musical composition, for which copyright has been obtained, without the consent of the proprietor of the said dramatic or musical composition, or his heirs or assigns, shall be liable for damages therefor, such damages in all cases to be assessed at such sum, not less than one hundred dollars for the first and fifty dollars for every subsequent performance, as to the Court shall appear to be just. If the unlawful performance and representation be wilful and for profit, such person or persons shall be guilty of a misdemeanor, and upon conviction be imprisoned for a period not exceeding one year. — U. S. Revised Statutes, Title 60, Chap. 3.

PR
4827
M35
1914

N. D. S. U. LIBRARY
FARGO N. D.

DEDICATION

TO MISS MARIE TEMPEST

Dear Marie Tempest:

An author who has spent many months in the perplexing business of constructing and writing a play naturally grows tired of it as soon as, or even before, it is produced. It is a tribute to your delightful performance of Mary Whichello that, though I find a decreasing interest in watching the play, I find an increasing pleasure in watching your performance.

In every play it matters little what the author has conceived and written, if it is not vitalized by the actor. It is only that part of a play, or that part of a character, which is thus vitalized by the acting — it is only this which counts with an audience.

How wonderfully you have vitalized every moment of Mary Whichello! How right is every accent, how clearly cut every gesture, how significant every movement, every glance, every look! What a happy

[v]

51074

vivacity of mischief, what a fascinating, busy energy there is about it all, like that of some pretty butterfly suddenly become industrious!

You seem to have a perpetual enjoyment in your art. It isn't work; it is just a pleasurable activity, which infects all who watch it. In these days of long runs, how often does one notice a decline of the actor's interest in his work after the first few weeks of a successful play. The general performance is apt to grow stale and perfunctory. If it is a comedy, it is forced into a noisy farce; if it is a serious drama, it loses its freshness and sincerity of feeling. But an impersonation of yours continuously retains its first bright, eager impulse; it remains spontaneous to the end, and kindles a responsive sympathy of laughter and emotion as surely on the last night as on the first.

Gratefully and admiringly yours,

Henry Arthur Jones

INTRODUCTION

Mary Goes First is an example of a type of drama which has not as yet, to any great extent, been cultivated in America; for this type — which is commonly called High Comedy — requires for its inspiration a social tradition that has been handed down for centuries. It has frequently been said that it takes three generations to make a gentleman; but it takes more than three to develop a Comedy of Manners. Manners do not become a theme for satire until they have been crystallized into a code; and, to laugh politely, a playwright must have an aristocracy to laugh at. The spirit of our people is inexorably opposed to the very idea of an aristocracy of birth: we cannot have an aristocracy of wealth, since the phrase itself presents an irresoluble contradiction in terms; and we have hardly yet had time to develop an aristocracy of culture. To all intents and purposes, the United States is still a country without an upper class; and the chaos of our social system precludes the possibility of social satire in our native drama. As Mr. Walter Prichard Eaton has pithily remarked, most of our American comedies must be classed as Comedies of Bad Manners. We laugh uproariously at impoliteness on our stage, because we have not yet learned to laugh delicately at politeness. We are amused at the eccentricities of bad behavior, because we have not yet learned to be amused at the eccentricities of good behavior.

High Comedy is the last of all dramatic types to be established in the art of any nation; and until we have had time to develop a native Comedy of Manners, we must content ourselves with an appreciation of the social satires of our somewhat elder cousins overseas. In this particular domain of art, America is still a province of Great Britain.

Among contemporary British dramatists, no other has been so signally successful in the handling of High Comedy as Mr. Henry Arthur Jones. In a notable series of comedies — among which may be mentioned *The Liars*, *The Case of Rebellious Susan*, *The Manœuvres of Jane*, *Whitewashing Julia*, *Joseph Entangled*, and *Dolly Reforming Herself* — he has satirized the foibles of the British aristocracy. Most of these pieces were originally presented at the Criterion Theatre, in London, which is perhaps the most aristocratic playhouse in the English-speaking world; and the author enjoyed the initial advantage of setting up a mirror before the very people who applauded his compositions from the stalls.

In selecting the characters for *Mary Goes First*, the author has descended a rung or two on the ladder of social precedence. Instead of exhibiting aristocrats, he has chosen to present people who are merely ambitious of aristocracy; and he makes fun of their innate inability to conform with the code of conduct which is an obligation of that nobility to which they ineffectually aspire. These people — to define them with a word that was lifted into literature by the late Clyde Fitch — are social "climbers"; and they are funny mainly because they fail to understand the principle that *noblesse oblige*.

Though we have no knighthoods and no baronetcies in America, and though we seldom trouble our minds about the order of a procession to the dinner-table, this struggle for social and political precedency in a small industrial city suggests many recognizable counterparts in our own habitual experience; and Mr. Jones's satire is, in this case, nearly as applicable to life in the United States as it is to life in England.

From the artistic standpoint, *Mary Goes First* must be regarded as a very notable achievement. In High Comedy, it is desirable that the incidents should seem to issue inevitably from the characters; and this piece is almost utterly a comedy of character rather than a comedy of incident. All who are familiar with the serious dramas of Mr. Jones must agree that one of his greatest gifts for the theatre is the faculty for story-telling; yet, in this comedy, he has managed artfully to make his effect with scarcely any story. The piece narrates a single incident — which, in itself, is trivial — and exhibits the subsequent effect of this single incident on the characters of all the people to whom it seems momentous. The plot of the play is purely psychological; and the action is developed not so much upon the stage as within the minds of the comically unimportant people who regard their destinies as hanging upon minor matters which the audience perceives to be absurd.

Attention should be directed to the technical dexterity which is displayed in the staging of this comedy. The entire piece is set forth in a single room — a room, moreover, which has only one door that is available for entrances and exits. To be sure, an adjoining room is partially displayed behind an opening that is hung with curtains, and this secondary room is employed as a means for the temporary withdrawal of certain characters from participation in the dialogue; but there is only one door through which the story — so to speak — is afforded communication with the outside world. This constricted stage-set was, of course, suggested to the author by the exigencies of his final curtain-fall. To accentuate the effect of what may be called — in the slang of the theatre — the "biggest laugh" of the comedy, it was necessary that there should be only one available exit from the scene; but so naturally has Mr. Jones arranged the entrances and exits of his characters that the hasty reader might not even notice that a scarcely precedented technical difficulty had, in this case, been accepted and surmounted.

No less admirable, in illustration of sheer craftsmanship, is what may be called the "time-scheme" of this play. Consider, for example, the novel advantage which the author has derived, in the middle of his first act, from the device, now generally accepted in the theatre, of lowering the curtain for a few seconds to indicate a lapse of time. By applying this device to indicate the passing of the dinner-hour, Mr. Jones has managed deftly to separate his women from his men, so that the altercation between Mary and Lady Bodsworth may take place in a purely feminine environment, before the men return from table. Consider also the cleverness of inventing a dressmaking establishment to account for the necessary minutes spent off-stage by Mary in Act II, and the skill with which Mr. Jones has brought the club, the railway-station, and many other off-stage localities, as clearly into the total map of his narrative as the single room which we actually see.

Since this is a comedy of character, and since there is very little physical action to illustrate the contrasted personalities, the burden of the comedy must be borne almost entirely by the dialogue. This dialogue is written with a literary mastery that can be appreciated only by those who are familiar with the requirements of the stage. Prof. Brander Matthews has distinguished three types of witticism in the drama, — the wit of words, the wit of situation, and the wit of character. Of these three types, the ʳudest and most easy is the first, and the most difficult and most artistic is the last. A verbal witticism is quotable apart from its context, and is therefore not inherent in the situation or the character; but the funniest lines in comedy are never quotable, because their humor is dependent on the fact that they are said in a certain situation or by a certain person. In the entire dialogue of *Mary Goes First* there is scarcely a line that could be quoted as funny in itself, because of its formula of words; and yet the dialogue as a whole is unfalteringly funny, because of the people who speak the lines, and the situations which inspire them. The word "improper" is by no means funny in itself; and yet whenever, in the later acts of this comedy, it trembles on the lips of the heroine, we laugh heartily at the reminiscence of a phrase in which the word was first singled out to our attention.

The final touch of art that must be noted in this comedy is its apparent simplicity and naturalness. As Mr. Max Beerbohm has remarked, in appreciation of the craftsmanship of Mr. Henry Arthur Jones, "We are not made conscious of it while the play is in progress. From the very outset we are aware merely of certain ladies and gentlemen behaving with apparent freedom and naturalness. It is only when the play is over that we notice the art of it."

CLAYTON HAMILTON.

The following is the cast of the comedy as it was first performed at the Playhouse, London, under the management of Miss Marie Tempest.

To-night, Thursday, September 18th, 1913, at 7.30, and every following Evening at 8.30

Miss MARIE TEMPEST will present, for the First Time, a New and Original Comedy, called

MARY GOES FIRST
By HENRY ARTHUR JONES

Thus it appears that the Honours and Dignities adjudged by the State serve often but to vanish the Stratagems and Pretences whereby they have been obtained; and the claim to Precedency is shewn to be the claim of those who have no other claim to our Admiration and Esteem.—FETTLEWORTH'S *Credentials of Merit* (1764), Chapter on Titles.

SIR THOMAS BODSWORTH .	MR. KENYON MUSGRAVE
RICHARD WHICHELLO . .	MR. CHARLES V. FRANCE
FELIX GALPIN . . .	MR. W. GRAHAM BROWNE
MR. TADMAN	MR. GEORGE SHELTON
DR. CHESHER	MR. HERBERT ROSS
HARVEY BETTS (*one of the Junior Liberal Whips*) .	MR. RICHARD LLUELLYN
POLLARD	MR. JOHN ALEXANDER
DAKIN	MR. HORTON COOPER
LADY BODSWORTH . . .	MISS HAMLEY CLIFFORD
ELLA SOUTHWOOD . . .	MISS MARGARET BRÜHLING
MRS. TADMAN	MISS CLAIRE PAUNCEFORT
and	
MARY (MRS.) WHICHELLO	MISS MARIE TEMPEST

The Play produced by Mr. W. GRAHAM BROWNE

[xiv]

MARY GOES FIRST
Act 1

PERSONS REPRESENTED

Sir Thomas Bodsworth, knight.
Richard Whichello.
Felix Galpin.
Mr. Tadman.
Dr. Chesher.
Harvey Betts, one of the Junior Liberal Whips.
Pollard.
Dakin.

Lady Bodsworth.
Mary Whichello.
Ella Southwood.
Mrs. Tadman.

The scene is laid throughout in Felix Galpin's house, at Saint John's Hill, the "residential" suburb of the manufacturing town of Warkinstall.

ACT I

SCENE: *Drawing-room at* FELIX GALPIN'S, *on an evening in early January. At the back, left, is a wide opening, hung with curtains, which are open and give a view of a further room. In the right corner at back is a door. On the right side in the centre is a large fireplace. On the left side down stage is a bow window. The rooms are brightly and comfortably furnished in a modern style. There is an absence of feminine knick-knacks. Nothing indicates very good or very bad taste in the occupier. Everything is ordinary and unobtrusive; the furniture is such as would be carelessly chosen by a young professional man from the best shop in a large provincial town. A card-table open, with packs of cards and bridge markers, is at the back. A bright fire is burning and the room is well lighted and looks cheerful. A few flowers on the shelf, and a large, handsome bouquet on a table, left.*

Discover: DAKIN *the butler.* *Enter* DR. CHESHER, *a Harley Street physician, about sixty, in evening dress.*

CHESHER. Mr. Galpin back from the office yet?

DAKIN. Yes, sir. He arrived just after you had gone up to dress. Here he is, sir.

Enter FELIX GALPIN, *a good-looking young lawyer, rather over thirty; smart, amiable, good-tempered; a very engaging personality. He is in evening dress, with a very rare orchid in his buttonhole.*

FELIX [*Advancing cordially to* CHESHER, *shaking hands*]. Ah, my dear Uncle! How are you?

CHESHER. Excellent!

FELIX [*To* DAKIN]. Dakin, get on to the champagne with the fish. Keep the glasses filled.

DAKIN. Yes, sir. [*Going.*

FELIX. And Dakin, when you announce Sir Thomas and Lady Bodsworth, throw it up a bit — [*illustrating*] — "Sir Thomas and Lady Bodsworth." Like that!

DAKIN. Yes, sir. [*Exit.*

FELIX. He only got his knighthood last week, and she was a grocer's daughter; so they'll like

[4]

to hear their title rolled out. Well, my dear Uncle, it's awfully good of you to run down to this hole ——

CHESHER. How are things looking?

FELIX. Thundering bad. The Warkinstall people are too busy to go to law. They spend all their time making portmanteaus and harness instead of going to law and doing me a good turn. I've only had one job for a fortnight.

CHESHER. But the practice was a good one when you bought it.

FELIX. It had gone down. And when my predecessor died, old Tadman nipped in and collared the best part of it.

CHESHER [Looking round]. But you've taken this big house in the best suburb — and you're giving dinner parties ——

FELIX. All the best people, such as they are, live in St. John's Hill. So I took this house, dine them, go to church regularly, fuss up all the old dowagers, play cricket and lawn tennis with the young people, subscribe to all their confounded charities, just to get in with them all.

CHESHER. In order to arrive, you show everybody that you have arrived.

FELIX. That's it. But if I don't arrive very soon I shall have to change my point of view, chuck the Tories and Church people, and go in a mucker for dissent and radicalism.

CHESHER. Will that be necessary?

FELIX. It's absolutely necessary that I shouldn't starve. My income last year was eighty-six pounds. I've got seven pounds in the bank, and I haven't paid for to-night's dinner party. Isn't it about time I changed my political principles?

CHESHER. It is better to change one's political principles than to starve.

FELIX. Oh, if it comes to *principles*, my *principles* are thoroughly Tory — so far as they go. Especially as in Warkinstall all the nicest people are Tories.

CHESHER. The present member is a Tory, isn't he?

FELIX. Elkington? Yes, Elkington is a strong Tory.

CHESHER. The object of going into politics being to get something out of it, the question for a sensible man is which party he can get most out of.

FELIX. Just so. And I should have turned over to the Radicals before this only ——

[6]

CHESHER. Only?

FELIX. I've lately got very friendly with the Whichellos.

CHESHER. The Whichellos?

FELIX. They're quite the best people in Warkinstall, rather a different cut from the rest. He's a big manufacturer here, and a very decent fellow. Mrs. Whichello is the leader of Warkinstall society — if you can call it Society. She bosses everything in Warkinstall — or she has bossed everything up to now. But now old Bodsworth has got this title — he's another big manufacturer and the Mayor of Warkinstall — he has just built a barn of a sanatorium, and got this knighthood for it ——

CHESHER. Oh, yes. I saw his name in the New Year's honors last week — very low down.

FELIX. Well, low down or not, he has got his knighthood. And jolly hard he and Lady Bodsworth have worked to get it — out of a Liberal Government. I don't think the Whichellos will quite like it, Mrs. Whichello especially. She's a delightful little woman, but she does like to play first fiddle. Oh, doesn't she? And now I expect Lady Bodsworth will want to have a look-in.

CHESHER. They're coming to-night?

[7]

FELIX. Yes, the Whichellos, the Bodsworths, the Tadmans, and — Miss Southwood.

CHESHER. Miss Southwood?

FELIX. Mrs. Whichello's sister — such a charming girl — in fact, well — I'm engaged to her.

CHESHER. On eighty-six pounds a year?

FELIX. Ella has a little money of her own. We aren't formally engaged, except between our two selves. But Mrs. Whichello is on our side, and I don't think Whichello will stand out. Ella is only nineteen, and Whichello is her guardian. That's the reason I haven't gone over to the Radicals.

CHESHER. Why?

FELIX. Whichello is a Tory, and very strong on Tariff Reform, so I've got to keep in with him. And I thought if only I can manage to hang on for a year or two with the Tories and Church people — Tadman's getting old and groggy — he may pop off some day ——

CHESHER. What is the amount of Miss Southwood's fortune?

FELIX. Five or six hundred a year. But I don't want to sponge on her. And if you'd stand by me for a bit — you've been such a good friend — I don't like to ask you, but ——

[8]

CHESHER. All right, my dear boy, I'll see what I can do.

FELIX. Thanks. It's awfully good of you. And now you're down here, you might give me a lift with the Bodsworths.

CHESHER. How?

FELIX. Bodsworth's sanatorium is going to pot. They've killed a patient with radium. He was a favorite curate ——

CHESHER. Seems a drastic measure to take — even with a curate.

FELIX. Then Bodsworth is very keen on hot water. And he's having ructions with the doctors about the treatment. Then just as he gets his knighthood, there's a blazing scandal about a young house surgeon and one of the nurses — I've asked him to show you over the sanatorium to-morrow morning.

CHESHER. Thank you. What for?

FELIX. Well, as you're a leading London physician, he'll be flattered. You might buck him up about his hot-water treatment — he may be having a lawsuit with the doctors ——

CHESHER. In that case, I should probably be on the side of the doctors.

[9]

FELIX. But hot water must be a cure for some diseases. Isn't it?

CHESHER. As a panacea it's about equal to most other cures.

FELIX. Well, there you are. And you can praise the situation — the salubrious air and the magnificent view — miles and miles of heather — and I say, I've put you next to Lady Bodsworth at dinner tonight — of course I take her in — you sit next ——

CHESHER. What subject of conversation would be congenial to her?

FELIX. Oh, the knighthood. You needn't talk about anything else. She has only been "my lady" a week. I'm giving this little dinner in honor of the event. I got that bouquet down from Covent Garden to present to her.

CHESHER [*Smelling*]. Gorgeous!

FELIX. Isn't it?

CHESHER. Looks almost equal to a baronetcy.

FELIX [*Listening, taking out watch*]. There's a motor just driven up. You haven't congratulated me about Ella.

CHESHER. I do, most heartily.

FELIX. Wait till you see her. I wish for her sake I'd gone in for politics instead of the law, especially

[10]

now there's four hundred a year to start with. My old Charterhouse chum, Harvey Betts, has just been made Junior Whip to the Liberal Party.

CHESHER. So I see in the papers this morning.

FELIX. When Harvey was at Oxford he was the fiercest young Tory. Russian despotism was too mild for him.

CHESHER. When a man talks that kind of nonsense at twenty, you know he'll talk the other kind of nonsense before he's forty.

Enter DAKIN.

DAKIN [*Announces*]. Miss Southwood.

ELLA *enters in evening dress, an attractive modern girl of nineteen.   Exit* DAKIN.

FELIX. How d'ye do?   [*Shaking hands.*]

ELLA. Oh, Mr. Galpin, Mary has sent me on to say that she and Dick may be a few minutes late. Will you excuse them?

FELIX. Certainly.   [*Introducing.*] My uncle, Dr. Chesher, Miss Southwood.

CHESHER. How d'ye do?   [*Shaking hands.*]

ELLA. How d'ye do?   Is this your first visit to Warkinstall?

[11]

CHESHER. Yes. I've not been able to get away since my nephew has settled here.

ELLA. I hope you'll come again. [*To* FELIX.] Mary has given me a message for you —— [*Slightly glancing at* CHESHER.]

CHESHER [*Taking the hint*]. Felix, I've got a telegram to send. Will you excuse me?

> [*Exit* CHESHER. FELIX *watches him off, then goes quickly to* ELLA *and snatches a kiss.*]

FELIX [*Very admiringly*]. You look charming!

ELLA. Do I? I've been so rushed — I had to throw my things on. Mary's terribly upset.

FELIX. What about?

ELLA. Lady Bodsworth.

FELIX. What's the matter?

ELLA. The woman has become quite insufferable. She does nothing but wallow in this knighthood.

FELIX. It is rather a dizzy honor. Give me another kiss — [*they kiss*] — and tell me all about Lady Bodsworth's wallowing.

ELLA. Her head's turned. She insists on patronizing Mary. Fancy any one patronizing Mary! There was quite a flare-up after the meeting this afternoon.

FELIX. Meeting?

[12]

ELLA. This Working Girls' Protection Society that they are getting up.

FELIX. Oh, yes — to look after the behavior of the factory girls.

ELLA. Well, it has been rather shocking. And last month the wives of the manufacturers met, and decided to form a Girls' Protection Society, and let all the factory girls know that they'd be expected to join.

FELIX. Kind of Mutual Moral Insurance Company.

ELLA. Mary took a lot of trouble, and naturally she expected to be made president.

FELIX. And wasn't she?

ELLA. No. Lady Bodsworth has worked the thing and this afternoon at the meeting she was elected president. And she positively gloated over Mary.

FELIX. Did she? Give me another kiss — [*snatching a kiss*] — and tell me what Mary did when Bodsworth gloated.

ELLA. She came home and nearly had hysterics.

FELIX. Nearly? I wonder she didn't quite. However, I suppose we shall have to let Lady Bodsworth gloat.

ELLA. No. Mary sent me on to say that as the knighthood has only been announced, and Mr. Bodsworth hasn't yet got the title, she supposes in strict etiquette you'll take her in to dinner to-night.

FELIX [*Aghast*]. Take her in to dinner ——?

ELLA. Mary wouldn't have raised the question with any one but you; but as you want to be engaged to me, she thinks you might oblige her.

FELIX. But how can I?

ELLA. It's very hard on Mary. She has always been taken in first at every dinner party in Warkinstall. Now Lady Bodsworth will always go first, so this will be the last time for poor Mary.

FELIX. Is she very keen on it?

ELLA. Well, she says she doesn't mind. But between ourselves she is simply furious at Lady Bodsworth's rudeness to her this afternoon.

FELIX. What on earth am I to do?

ELLA. He isn't actually knighted. It would be strict etiquette, wouldn't it?

FELIX. I don't know the strict etiquette of the thing, but I'm giving this dinner in honor of the knighthood. I've told Bodsworth so. And I've got that bouquet for Lady Bodsworth.

ELLA. Can't you explain to the Bodsworths?

FELIX. Good heavens, no! I should make them enemies for life. No, I must take in the old Bodsworth woman now!

Enter DAKIN, *announcing rather loudly, a little over-doing it.*

DAKIN. Sir Thomas and Lady Bodsworth.

Enter SIR THOMAS *and* LADY BODSWORTH. *Exit* DAKIN. LADY BODSWORTH *is about forty-five. She is rather stout and made up to look young. Her hair is obtrusively golden, very plentiful, and puffed out. Her complexion is artificial, and her cheeks bloom with a magenta tint. She is handsomely and showily dressed, with a good deal of jewelry. She is patronizing, fussy, self-conscious, self-satisfied, and beaming with amiability.* BODSWORTH *is a stolid, thick-set, rather pompous man about fifty, with large, immobile features; thick, coarse black hair turning gray; he is quite destitute of humor.* FELIX *advances very cordially to* LADY BODSWORTH *as* ELLA *shakes hands with* SIR THOMAS.

FELIX [*Shaking hands*]. My dear Lady Bodsworth, this is really good of you.

LADY B. We've been quite overwhelmed with invitations since Sir Thomas received his honor. Everybody seems so pleased that we have been recognized. We are lunching at Petbury Park on Tuesday.

FELIX. I'm in luck.

LADY B. I really think you are. We had three invitations for dinner to-night. But as we had accepted yours, we thought it wouldn't be honorable to put you off.

FELIX. Noblesse oblige!

LADY B. Quite so. Ah, Ella, my dear!

[*Goes to* ELLA *and kisses her very affectionately, talks with her.*]

FELIX. Sir Thomas, how are you?

SIR T. [*Shaking hands*]. Run off my legs. My own business — municipal business — church business — political business — and now this honor — really if people knew what it entailed they would scarcely envy me the distinction which it has pleased his Majesty to confer upon me.

CHESHER *has reëntered.*

FELIX [*Calling off* LADY BODSWORTH]. Lady Bodsworth, let me present my uncle, Dr. Chesher of Harley Street.

[16]

LADY B. I'm very pleased to meet you.

CHESHER [*Shaking hands*]. Delighted!

LADY B. Sir Thomas has just given a sanatorium to Warkinstall. From first to last it won't cost less than ——

SIR T. Shush, my dear. Whether it costs thirty thousand or forty thousand, what does it matter?

FELIX. My uncle is very much interested in hot water treatment —— [*With a little wink and an imploring look at* CHESHER.]

SIR T. [*Interested*]. Indeed! I'm sorry to say my present staff are very much prejudiced in favor of their own methods.

LADY B. Sir Thomas has derived so much benefit himself from hot water that he wishes all the patients to be given a chance.

FELIX [*Looking anxiously at* CHESHER]. My uncle says that in certain diseases hot water — eh, Uncle? In certain diseases ——?

CHESHER. It was extensively used by Gil Blas of Santillane when he practised in Seville.

SIR T. How did it answer in his case?

CHESHER. Several of his patients died. But that may have been a natural predisposition, such as a

[17]

doctor often encounters in his patients. And Gil Blas stuck to his treatment.

Sir T. Quite right. Is he in practice now?

Chesher. I'm afraid not — but his reputation remains.

Sir T. Because that's the kind of doctor I want at the head of my sanatorium.

Enter Dakin.

Dakin [*Announcing*]. Mr. and Mrs. Tadman.

Enter Mr. *and* Mrs. Tadman. *Exit* Dakin. Mrs. Tadman *is a pleasant, motherly, middle-class woman about sixty.* Tadman *is about seventy, with straggling white hair and a shiny, rosy complexion — gouty — shaky — tremulous.*

Felix [*Shaking hands*]. How d'ye do?

Mrs. T. How d'ye do?

Felix. So kind of you to come. [*To* Tadman.] How are you? [*Shaking hands.*]

Tadman. First rate — just as good a man as ever I was.

Felix. Then you'll be able to do justice to a bottle of port.

Tadman [*His eyes brighten, and he briskly rubs his*
[18]

decayed hands]. I'll try! I'll try! There's only one wine — [*with a little anticipatory smack of the lips*] — port! Sir Thomas, I hope you won't change your principles on Tariff Reform.

Sir T. Change my principles on Tariff Reform?

Tadman. Now the Liberal Government has honored you.

Sir T. The Liberal Government makes a very great mistake if it supposes that I am to be bought by a knighthood.

Tadman [*Comes closer to him, glances at* Ella, *who is talking to* Mrs. Tadman]. I hear that Whichello is wobbling over the food taxes ——

Sir T. Yes, and he's siding with the Radicals against me over the cemetery and the tramways extension.

Enter Dakin.

Dakin [*Announcing*]. Mr. and Mrs. Whichello.
[*Exit* Dakin.

[Mrs. Whichello *is a piquant, attractive little lady, rather under thirty. She has the air of one accustomed to be first in her own circle. She is clever enough to get her own way by finesse and persuasion when she cannot command*

[19]

*it by authority — a very determined little crea-
ture. She is charmingly but very quietly
dressed in a well-made gown. Her hair is
done very plainly and neatly. She wears
one very handsome pearl and diamond neck-
lace, and no other jewelry, except a wedding
ring. She shows suppressed excitement from
the afternoon quarrel with* LADY BODSWORTH.
*She is evidently full of mischief, ripe for an
explosion, and is preserving her self-control
with difficulty.* DICK WHICHELLO *is a good
looking, very ordinary Englishman of the
better classses; rather over thirty-five, getting
stout and lazy; something of the sporting
type; very casual, amiable, and easy going as a
rule, but very obstinate and hot-tempered when
he is provoked.*]

FELIX [*Very cordially to* MARY]. **Delightful of**
you to spare me an evening. [*Shaking hands.*] **How**
are you? No need to ask. [*Turning to* DICK, *shaking hands.*] How are you?

DICK. Splendid.

FELIX [*Introducing*]. **Dr. Chesher, Mrs. Which-**
ello.

MARY [*Shaking hands with* CHESHER]. How d'ye do?

CHESHER. Very pleased to meet you.

FELIX [*Introducing*]. Mr. Whichello—Dr. Chesher.

[DICK *and* CHESHER *shake hands and talk.* MARY *nods and smiles to* MRS. TADMAN, *who returns the nod and smile.*]

MARY [*To* TADMAN]. How d'ye do? [*Shaking hands.*]

TADMAN. Growing younger every day.

MARY [*Bowing to* SIR THOMAS]. Sir Thomas, I have congratulated you on your honor, haven't I?

SIR T. [*Very stiffly*]. Thank you, you have congratulated me three times during the past week.

MARY. Have I? [*Very sweetly.*] Oh, I really must give myself the pleasure of congratulating you once more. May I?

SIR T. [*Shows resentment*]. If you wish, but — really I ——

[*Turns to* LADY BODSWORTH, *who stands looking at* MARY, *maliciously triumphant. There is an awkward pause as the two women look at each other.* MARY *bows very distantly to* LADY BODSWORTH. LADY BODSWORTH

[21]

barely inclines her head. FELIX *watches apprehensively and tries to smooth the unpleasantness.*]

FELIX [*To* LADY BODSWORTH]. Mrs. Whichello, like all of us, feels she cannot sufficiently express her congratulations to her old friends, eh, Mrs. Whichello?

MARY. Yes, that's it.

FELIX [*To* MARY]. And I'm sure Lady Bodsworth is equally pleased to receive your congratulations.

LADY B. Oh, I've no wish to be unfriendly. I'm quite ready to forget our little tiff this afternoon if she is.

MARY. Oh, quite.

LADY B. [*Patronizingly*]. You and Mr. Whichello must come and lunch with us some day.

MARY. We *shall* feel honored. Shan't we, Dick?

DICK. Yes, delighted!

LADY B. Shall we say Tuesday? No, I forgot. On Tuesday Sir Thomas and I are lunching at Petbury Park. The Countess saw me yesterday in the High Street. She stopped her motor instantly, and gave me the most pressing invitation.

MARY. The dear Countess!

LADY B.   She was so hearty in her congratulations. She said, "Come on Tuesday.   Petbury and I shall be quite alone, and we shall have you all to ourselves."

MARY.   How delightful for you!   And for them!

LADY B.   So it can't be Tuesday.   Shall we say Wednesday?

MARY.   May I look at my book when I get home?

LADY B.   Certainly.   Name your own day, and remember that for the future I shan't bear any ill-feeling; and I hope you won't.

MARY.   Ill-feeling!   My dear Lady Bodsworth, I'm only too thankful for your sake that this dreadful scandal at the sanatorium wasn't made public before the New Year's honors were announced.

SIR T.   Why?   What difference would it have made?

MARY.   Well, with such disgraceful behavior going on in your beautiful new building before the walls were scarcely dry, it would have made it very difficult for the Government to reward you for your noble gift to the town.

SIR T.   [*Very stiffly*].   I don't see that.   We needn't discuss the matter.

[23]

MARY. No, no. Better keep it quiet. I hope there's nothing more to come out ——

SIR T. We have made a thorough inquiry, and the affair is terminated.

MARY. I'm so glad you've managed to hush it up. [*To* LADY BODSWORTH.] What have you done with the nurse?

SIR T. [*Very stiffly*]. We have expelled her.

MARY. Quite right. Quite right. I hope you made her feel that her shocking conduct has shed quite a blight over the general rejoicing.

SIR T. Not at all! Not at all!

MARY. It has shed a blight on my rejoicing. I can never go by your beautiful sanatorium now without dreading that the nurses and doctors are ——

SIR T. [*Interrupting*]. We need not pursue the subject.

MARY. No, no. The less said the better. But I always distrusted her yellow hair. I've invariably noticed that when a woman has that peculiar shade of hair, and especially when she dresses it in that ridiculous towzly fashion—— [*She sees the expression on* SIR THOMAS's *face and she makes a feigned gesture of intense vexation.*] Oh, what have I said?

[24]

What have I said? My dear Lady Bodsworth!
How could I be so thoughtless!   How could I ——?
　　　[*Making little helpless appealing gestures of
　　　　apology to* LADY BODSWORTH *and to all the
　　　　company.*]

LADY B. [*Much offended*].   I hope you don't com-
pare me with a person of that class ——

MARY. No! No! A thousand apologies! Now,
do say you forgive me!

LADY B. [*Curtly*]. Oh, certainly.

MARY. Thank you.   I can't tell you how much I
admire your hair, no matter how it's done.   By and
by I shall ask you to tell me how you get that effect.
Now you will tell me, won't you?

LADY B. [*Curtly*]. Oh, it's quite simple.

MARY. Ah, it may be easy for you ——

FELIX [*Who has been very anxiously watching, in-
terposes*].   You mustn't discuss these delicate little
feminine secrets before us men. Mrs. Whichello,
you're passionately fond of flowers — what do you
think of these for early January? [*Draws* MARY *off
to the bouquet.*]

MARY [*Goes into raptures*].   Roses and carnations!
[*Takes up the bouquet, smells it, admires it.*]   Aren't
they exquisite? [*To* ELLA, *who has joined them.*]

[25]

ELLA. Perfectly lovely!

MARY [*Putting down the flowers*]. Did you give my message to Mr. Galpin?

ELLA. Yes. [*Looking at* FELIX.]

> [*They draw together and are seen to be talking eagerly.* MARY *is excited, and is urging her point of etiquette.* FELIX *is deprecatory, apologetic, explanatory, and persuasive.* LADY BODSWORTH *is talking to* MRS. TADMAN, *with angry glances at* MARY. MRS. TADMAN *is trying to soothe her.* SIR THOMAS, TADMAN, CHESHER, *and* DICK *are grouped together.*]

DICK. You must join our golf club, Sir Thomas.

SIR T. [*Shakes his head*]. Too busy — and now I've been recognized — it's a great burden — no time for golf.

DICK. He must make time, mustn't he, Doctor?

CHESHER. As a serious career golf is an excellent substitute for politics.

DICK. By Jove, yes. [*To* SIR THOMAS.] I shall put you up. We must have you. The fact is our present course is rotten. We want you to let us have that corner slope below the sanatorium.

[CHESHER *joins* LADY BODSWORTH *and* MRS. TADMAN.]

SIR T. I am about to enclose that slope in the sanatorium grounds for the benefit of my patients.

DICK. Oh, they can stroll about it. We really must have that slope.

SIR T. It's quite impossible. I'm a little surprised at your asking, after opposing me on the Town Council with regard to the tramways and the cemetery.

DICK. Oh, we must give the new town a decent cemetery.

SIR T. There is plenty of room in our venerable old churchyard. And I hope, when it pleases heaven to call me to itself, that what is mortal of me will repose in the shadow of our ancient parish church.

DICK. You don't want what is mortal of you to drain down into my factory, do you?

SIR T. [*Offended*]. I consider that remark as quite uncalled for — indeed, profane. I intend to oppose the cemetery and the tramway extension. Especially as both proposals emanate from the Radicals.

DICK. What does it matter where they emanate from, if they're for the good of the town?

SIR T. We must keep the control and administration of all these matters in our own hands. And I trust that as Chairman of the Conservative Party I may rely on your support.

[DICK *utters a little discontented grumble.*]

TADMAN. There's another thing, Whichello. We must have a thorough, complete, well-considered measure of Tariff Reform.

DICK. Oh, I'm a convinced Tariff Reformer, providing the leather trade is considered. But I'm hanged if I see how we're going to carry the food taxes.

TADMAN. It's absolutely necessary. It all hangs together. I've worked out a complete scheme. I can show you the figures.

SIR T. I hope, Whichello, you will reconsider your entire attitude. You are going the right way to split up the Conservative Party in Warkinstall.

[DICK *utters another discontented little growl. They go on discussing the matter.* CHESHER *has joined* LADY BODSWORTH *and* MRS. TADMAN. FELIX, MARY, *and* ELLA *have been talking among themselves.*]

MARY. I merely raised it as a point of strict etiquette.

FELIX. I wish I could — but —— [*Looks help-lessly at* ELLA.]

ELLA. I think you might have obliged Mary.

MARY [*Turning to the bouquet*]. It really doesn't matter. Aren't these flowers perfectly exquisite?

FELIX. I'm glad you like them.

MARY. I dote on roses and carnations. Now I'm sure you must have got them especially to please me, didn't you?

FELIX. Yes, I did. [*Glances at* LADY BODS-WORTH, *whose back is turned to them.*]

MARY [*To* ELLA]. Wasn't it kind of him? He knew how fond I was of roses and carnations. [*Smelling them.*]

FELIX [*Glances again at* LADY BODSWORTH's *back — hesitates — makes up his mind*]. Will you accept them? I sent up to Covent Garden especially to get them for you. [*Hands them to her.*]

MARY. How good of you! Dick! Look at these flowers! Mr. Galpin sent up to Covent Garden to get them especially for me.

> [*Goes to* MRS. TADMAN *and displays them in front of* LADY BODSWORTH, *who holds herself enviously aloof.*]

TADMAN [*Who has been arguing with* DICK]. No!

No! My scheme is elastic. It tightens over bacon in one place, and relaxes in another. The same with cheese! That's the beauty of it! It gives and takes.

[FELIX *has been talking to* ELLA, *looking at his watch, and glancing anxiously at the door.*]

FELIX. Sir Thomas, will you take in Mrs. Whichello? Whichello — Mrs. Tadman. [*To* TADMAN.] You'll look after Miss Southwood, won't you? Uncle, you'll have to bring up the rear. [*Joining* LADY BODSWORTH.] Lady Bodsworth, I am to have the privilege.

[*The couples sort themselves and talk apart.*]

LADY B. [*Enviously*]. What a lovely bouquet you presented to Mrs. Whichello.

FELIX. Um! Not bad. [*Dropping his voice and looking cautiously round to see that they are not overheard.*] I don't care much for roses and carnations.

LADY B. They are rather vulgar.

FELIX. One orchid is worth a ton of them. I wonder if you'd do me the honor to wear this —— [*Taking the orchid from his buttonhole.*]

LADY B. I shall be pleased. [*Looking enviously at* MARY's *bouquet.*]

[30]

FELIX. Can you fasten it?

LADY B. Yes, I think.

FELIX. An orchid is the aristocrat of flowers.

[*She places it in the neck of her dress, which is rather décolleté.*]

FELIX. That's a very rare variety. [*With a little half-wink at* ELLA, *who is watching.*] It's the first specimen to come to Warkinstall. [*Admiring it.*] Ah, now it shows to advantage!

Enter DAKIN.

DAKIN. Dinner is served, sir. [*Exit.*

MARY [*Replacing her bouquet in the vase*]. I'll put them there till I go home.

LADY B. [*Going off arm-in-arm with* FELIX—*speaking loudly so that* MARY *can hear*]. Yes, an orchid is such an aristocratic flower — so very aristocratic.

[*Exeunt* FELIX *and* LADY BODSWORTH.

SIR T. [*Going off with* MARY]. And he is also opposing me on the cemetery and the tramways.

MARY. Is he? [*Turning to* DICK, *who is just behind her.*] Dick, I'm surprised at you opposing Sir Thomas. [*To* SIR THOMAS.] I must talk to him very seriously.

[*Exeunt* SIR THOMAS *and* MARY.

Mrs. T. [*On* Dick's *arm*]. I don't quite understand Tariff Reform, but Mr. Tadman has worked it all out most carefully.

Dick. So have I, and I'm convinced that if we put on food taxes ——

[*Exit with* Mrs. Tadman *on his arm.*

Ella [*On* Tadman's *arm, turns round to* Chesher]. I wish there was another of me to come in with you, Dr. Chesher. [*Going off.*

Chesher. Ah! You'd be much safer with medicine than you are with the law.

[*He follows them off. The curtain falls for a few seconds to signify the passing of the dinner-time.*]

Scene II. *The same, after dinner. The curtains between the rooms have been drawn closely together.* Lady Bodsworth *and* Mrs. Tadman *are seated near to each other, and apart from* Mary *and* Ella. Mary *has her bouquet in her hand and is admiring it.* Ella *is turning over a book of views.*

Lady B. [*Expansively*]. We don't take it so much as an honor to ourselves as to the town.

Mrs. T. [*Toadying*]. That's what Mr. Tadman and I feel,

[32]

MARY [*Solemnly*]. That's what we all feel. Don't we, Ella?

ELLA. Oh, yes. Couldn't we have some fireworks over it?

MARY. Ella, please put away that book, and listen to Lady Bodsworth.

[ELLA *does so, and assumes an air of great interest in* LADY BODSWORTH.]

MARY. You were saying, dear Lady Bodsworth ——

LADY B. [*Ignoring* MARY, *speaks to* MRS. TADMAN]. That is how Sir Thomas and I wish it to be regarded — as an honor to everybody in Warkinstall.

MARY. Will it go round?

LADY B. Go round?

MARY. There are forty thousand people in Warkinstall. It's very unselfish of you, dear Lady Bodsworth, to share your honor amongst us, but — well, there won't be much for each of us, will there?

LADY B. [*Getting angry*]. Of course if you're annoyed ——

MARY. Annoyed? My dear Lady Bodsworth! My very dear Lady Bodsworth!

LADY B. [*To* MRS. TADMAN]. As it appears to

[33]

upset Mrs. Whichello, perhaps we'd better change the subject.

MARY. Oh, I love it! I could keep on all the evening.

LADY B. [*To* MRS. TADMAN]. We shall have a house in town for the season. Of course we shall have to go up when Sir Thomas receives ——

> [MARY *touches* ELLA's *arm with a solemn look of reproof, as if calling her to pay reverential attention to* LADY BODSWORTH. LADY BODSWORTH *stops, upset.*]

MARY [*After a pause of mock expectancy*]. When does Sir Thomas expect to be commanded —— ?

LADY B. I should really be obliged if you would choose some other topic of conversation.

MARY. Certainly, dear Lady Bodsworth. [*Very sweetly.*] And what shall we talk about now? Oh, yes! So you are lunching at Petbury Park?

LADY B. We are lunching at Petbury Park.

MARY. On Tuesday, isn't it?

LADY B. I believe I have already mentioned that fact.

MARY. Yes, but why not mention it again, dear Lady Bodsworth?

LADY B. Because it might cause you pain.

MARY. Pain? My dear Lady Bodsworth! Why should it cause me pain?

LADY B. You're not invited, I believe?

MARY. We couldn't expect it, as we dined there on Saturday.

LADY B. [*Upset*]. Dined! Oh! [*Nonplussed*.] Indeed!

MARY [*More sweetly than ever*]. And what shall we talk about now?

ELLA. I do think somebody ought to organize some fireworks ——

MARY [*Reprovingly*]. My dear Ella, it is not for you to choose a topic of conversation. We are waiting for Lady Bodsworth —— [*Looking at* LADY BODSWORTH *with an air of reverent expectancy.*]

LADY B. [*Looks at* MARY *with withering scorn, then magnificently ignores her, and speaks to* MRS. TADMAN]. Of course it's only natural that small minds should feel jealous when they see others selected for honor, when they themselves are left out in the cold. [*Just deigning to glance at* MARY.]

MARY. My dear Lady Bodsworth! My very dear Lady Bodsworth!

LADY B. There's no need to "Lady Bodsworth" me quite so often.

[35]

MARY. No?

> [LADY BODSWORTH *rises, draws herself up, and
> again looks at* MARY *with withering scorn.*]

LADY B. [*To* MRS. TADMAN]. I feel, dear, that
you would be more comfortable in the next room.

> [*Going toward curtains.*

MRS. T. [*Detaining her*]. Oh, I shouldn't take
any notice. I'm sure Mary wishes to remain friends,
don't you, Mary?

MARY. Oh, certainly. But if Lady Bodsworth
doesn't wish me to call her Lady Bodsworth, what
am I to call her?

MRS. T. You used always to call each other
"Fanny" and "Mary."

LADY B. It was quite at her own wish that I
called her "Mary."

MARY. If I remember rightly, dear Lady Bodsworth, you asked me to call you "Fanny"; and said
might you call me "Mary." And I replied, "Oh,
certainly!" Everybody in Warkinstall calls me
"Mary."

MRS. T. I don't suppose she'd mind if you called
her "Fanny."

MARY [*Looking mischievously at* LADY BODS-
WORTH]. I don't think I could call her "Fanny"—

now! Dear Lady Bodsworth, would you think it disrespectful if I called you "Fanny"?

LADY B. It's quite immaterial to me what you call me. Please yourself.

MARY [*Very sweetly*]. Thank you so much. [*A little pause.*] And what shall we talk about now — Fanny?

LADY B. [*Enraged, is about to explode; controls herself; tries to think of something very satirical, fails*]. I should much prefer that you didn't address any further remarks to me.

MARY. Very well, Fanny — [*checks herself*] — Lady Bodsworth.

LADY B. [*Seats herself with dignity and turns to* MRS. TADMAN *with the greatest amiability, speaks at* MARY]. How very nicely the meeting for the Girls' Protection Society passed off this afternoon!

MRS. T. Yes — very.

> [MARY *admonishes* ELLA *by a look to pay reverential attention to* LADY BODSWORTH.]

LADY B. I was so glad that they elected me as president; because I do feel that in my new position I shall be able to do so much to keep the poor girls out of temptation ——

> [MARY *utters a little gaspy shriek, pulls herself up, and looks demurely in front of her.*]

[37]

LADY B. Are you unwell, Mrs. Whichello?

MARY. Very nearly. Dear Lady Bodsworth, would you permit me to address one single remark to you?

LADY B. [*Suspiciously*]. Oh, certainly.

MARY [*Very respectful*]. Don't you think, dear Lady Bodsworth, that these poor factory girls, with their love of finery, and making the most of themselves — don't you think, if they are allowed to see very much of you, they may be tempted to imitate ——

LADY B. Imitate what?

MARY [*Glancing at* LADY BODSWORTH'S *coiffure*]. Those tresses ——

LADY B. [*Gathers herself up for a great burst of indignation*]. I have never been so insulted — I will not endure these insinuations! [*Splutters like a damp firework.*] Really I — just when everybody is so pleased that we've been honored — really I — [*crying a little*] — I will not —— [*recovers herself*]. But I can quite understand your feeling so spiteful at not being elected president ——

MARY. Spiteful, dear Lady Bodsworth?

LADY B. But I wouldn't show it. It's so small, so very small! I wouldn't be small if I were you!

MARY. Oh, if it comes to our figures — [*glancing at her own and* LADY BODSWORTH'S] — I'm very well satisfied.

LADY B. [*Magnificently indignant*]. I will thank you not to make any further remarks *to* me or *about* me!

MARY. Very well, dear Lady Bodsworth!

LADY B. [*To* MRS. TADMAN]. I'm sorry you should be exposed to all this annoyance. But we needn't put up with it any longer. [*Beckons to* MRS. TADMAN *to follow her off at curtains; then turns to* MARY *very spitefully*.] But you weren't elected president, were you?

> [*Exit through curtains.* MRS. TADMAN *has risen, a little embarrassed.*]

MRS. T. [*In a low tone to* MARY]. We all thought as Sir Thomas had just been knighted, it would be a pretty compliment to elect her as president. I hope you don't mind ——

MARY. Mind? My dear Mrs. Tadman! But those poor factory girls! Keep them out of temptation? Why, with her powdered cheeks and her yellow hair, she looks like an impropriety herself!

LADY B. [*Comes through the curtains, overwhelmed*]. Oh! oh! oh!

SIR THOMAS *enters, followed at short intervals by*
CHESHER, DICK, TADMAN *and* FELIX.

SIR T. What's the matter?

LADY B. I have never been so insulted ——

SIR T. Insulted?

LADY B. Mrs. Whichello called me ——

SIR T. What?

LADY B. [*Crying a little*]. She said I was — Mrs.
Tadman, you heard ——

SIR T. What did she call you?

LADY B. I couldn't repeat the word. We had
better go home at once.   [*Going toward door.*

FELIX [*Stopping her*]. No, Lady Bodsworth ——
[*Tries to soothe her.*]

DICK. Mary, what's this?

MARY. Nothing. I made a remark to Mrs.
Tadman. Lady Bodsworth was in the next room.
I didn't know she was listening. I'm sorry.

SIR T. Sorry? I wish to know what term you
have applied to Lady Bodsworth. [*There is a pause.*]

FELIX. Sir Thomas, Mrs. Whichello has said she
was sorry — I trust ——

SIR T. I insist on knowing the exact term which
has been applied to Lady Bodsworth. Fanny!

[40]

[*Calls* LADY BODSWORTH *aside, questions her, and is seen to be shocked, and indignant.* DICK *questions* MARY, *and is seen to show annoyance.* TADMAN *questions* MRS. TAD- MAN. FELIX *waits to question* TADMAN; *when* TADMAN *has received the information,* FELIX *calls him aside, and questions him.* CHESHER *joins them.* ELLA *slips quietly between the curtains into the next room.*]

DICK [*Having questioned* MARY, *in a tone of an- noyance*]. You oughtn't to have said it.

MARY. It slipped out.

DICK. Oh!

MARY. I tell you it slipped out.

DICK. Bodsworth, as an old friend I'm sure you won't take any notice of this ——

SIR T. Not take any notice? Do I understand, Whichello, that you approve of your wife calling Lady Bodsworth an impropriety?

DICK. Certainly not, but ——

SIR T. Then perhaps you will ask her to make a full and ample apology. [*Looks threateningly at* MARY.]

DICK. [*Prompting*]. Mary!

MARY. I'm extremely sorry ——

SIR T. Sorry? My wife an impropriety! The thing's monstrous!

FELIX. I'm sure Mrs. Whichello didn't use the word in any objectionable sense. It is a term that is often used in playful badinage —which I'm quite sure is all Mrs. Whichello intended.

SIR T. I don't care what Mrs. Whichello intended. I am waiting for her to apologize. [*Looks threateningly at* MARY. *A longish pause.*]

MARY [*Very simply and sincerely*]. I am extremely sorry, Lady Bodsworth.

LADY B. "Sorry" isn't an apology, is it?

FELIX. Oh, yes, it's quite equivalent, especially as Mrs. Whichello said it — with such genuine regret. Now that's passed over. Can we get up a rubber at bridge? [*Moving toward the card-table.*]

SIR T. I do not play bridge, and I do not consider that it has passed over. [*Looking at* LADY BODSWORTH.]

LADY B. It's such a flagrant offence. I couldn't pass it over without an apology.

FELIX. Mrs. Whichello, may I offer your sincere regrets, shall we say apologies, to Lady Bodsworth?

[LADY BODSWORTH *looks very triumphantly at* MARY — *there is again a long pause.*]

[42]

MARY. Certainly.

FELIX. There, Lady Bodsworth! That is very satisfactory, and we can all be friends again. Tadman, I know you're longing for a rubber —— [*Again moving toward card-table.*]

LADY B. [*Keeping her position, looking maliciously triumphant at* MARY]. It's so very flagrant. I should prefer an apology in writing — in case it might happen again. [*Looking at* SIR THOMAS.]

SIR T. Certainly — you're quite right. An apology in writing. [*Looking at* MARY.] Will that be forthcoming?

MARY [*Very decisively*]. No!

SIR T. Oh! Then do I understand that you call Lady Bodsworth an impropriety, and refuse to apologize?

MARY. I did not call Lady Bodsworth an impropriety. I said she looked like an impropriety. [*Looking intently at* LADY BODSWORTH, *speaking very deliberately, slowly driving each word home.*] She does not look like an impropriety — [*looking* LADY BODSWORTH *up and down*] — not the least like an impropriety.

LADY B. Oh — oh — Sir Thomas, will you please have our motor called?

[43]

Sir T. One moment, Fanny. Tadman, I shall place this matter in your hands. You will please draw up a form of apology; make it very stringent, and submit it to me.

Tadman. Yes — yes, Sir Thomas — but as I am also Whichello's legal adviser, I can act for both of you.

Sir T. You can act for me or for Mr. Whichello; but in this instance I prefer to have my own lawyer.

Tadman. You'd better let me arrange. I should advise Mrs. Whichello to retract ——

Mary. Thank you, Mr. Tadman, we prefer to have our own lawyer.

Dick. No, no, Mary. [*Is seen to be arguing with her.*]

Sir T. You will oblige me, Tadman, by saying whether you intend to act for Mr. Whichello or for me.

Tadman. Oh, for you, Sir Thomas, of course — but ——

Sir T. Very well. If Galpin will kindly excuse you, we will take our measures at once. Mrs. Tadman had better come with us while the exact words that Mrs. Whichello used are fresh in her mind. I'm sorry to break up your party, Galpin ——

FELIX. I'm sorry for the reason, Sir Thomas. [*To* LADY BODSWORTH.] But can't I persuade you ——

LADY B. I couldn't think of remaining in the company of —— [*Looking indignantly at* MARY.] I'll wait downstairs, please, till our motor is ready.

FELIX [*Offers his arm*]. Allow me. I'm sure Mrs. Whichello didn't intend —— [*Going off.*

LADY B. Oh, please don't mention her name.

[FELIX *takes off* LADY BODSWORTH. *The* TADMANS *are saying good-night and shaking hands with* DICK *and* MARY.]

SIR T. [*To* CHESHER]. Good-night, Doctor. [*Shaking hands.*] My wife an impropriety! What is your opinion of that?

CHESHER. A very obvious error in classification.

SIR T. My wife an impropriety! [*Getting more angry.* The more I think of it, the more monstrous it seems! [*Impatiently.*] Now, Tadman. if you're ready —— [*Exit.*

MRS. T. [*To* CHESHER]. Good-night ——

CHESHER. Let me see you to the motor. [*Takes off* MRS. TADMAN.]

TADMAN [*Shaking hands with* DICK]. Very sorry

[45]

— but as Sir Thomas is my oldest client — I'm sure you'll understand ——

MARY. Oh, we quite understand. [*Exit* TADMAN.

DICK. You've let me in for a pretty thing now ——

MARY. You surely don't want me to apologize ——

DICK. You'll have to one way or the other.

MARY. Indeed I shall not! Sign an apology for that woman to take about Warkinstall and show all my friends!

DICK. I'm not going to have a lawsuit. I shall go round to Tadman in the morning and get him to settle it.

MARY. Tadman? He's on their side. You can see that. I shall consult Mr. Galpin ——

FELIX *reënters.*

Oh, Mr. Galpin, I'm so sorry this has happened, but you'll be able to get us out of it, won't you?

Reënter CHESHER.

FELIX. I'll do my best, as a friend ——

MARY. No, we want you to act for us ——

FELIX. Mr. Tadman is Mr. Whichello's lawyer ——

MARY. Then you'll have to be mine.

FELIX. If Mr. Whichello wishes, but ——

DICK. I'm not going to have a lawsuit.

FELIX. I'll take very good care you don't, if I handle the case.

MARY. There, Dick! And I'm not going to apologize.

FELIX. There'll be no necessity, if I handle the case.

MARY. There, Dick! [DICK *utters a low, discontented growl.* MARY *goes to him.*] Now, Dick, don't be unreasonable. Mr. Galpin will arrange it so that I don't apologize, and that you don't have a lawsuit! [*Is seen to be arguing with him.*]

CHESHER [*In a low voice to* FELIX]. How are you going to manage it?

FELIX. I'm hanged if I know. [*To* MARY.] It isn't very late. Shall we have just one rubber?

MARY. Oh, do!

[FELIX *wheels the card-table into the centre of the room.*]

FELIX. Uncle, you'll take a hand. I'm very sorry, Mrs. Whichello, that you and Whichello have had such an uncomfortable evening.

[47]

MARY. Oh, I've enjoyed it thoroughly. Haven't you, Dick? [DICK *growls very discontentedly in his armchair.*] Dick, come up to the table and behave yourself. If you don't, I shall have to go and stay with Aunt Henrietta again. You won't like that. She won't have you near the place. [DICK *growls again.*]

FELIX [*Spreading out a pack*]. Shall we cut?

MARY [*Cuts*]. Now, Dick, come and cut, and think of something that will make you look happy!

DICK [*Rises, growls, comes to the table*]. What?

MARY. Think you've got to take me home in your motor car, while poor Sir Thomas has got to take Lady Bodsworth! [CHESHER *has cut.* DICK *has cut.*]

MARY [*Cuts*]. Two.

FELIX [*Cuts*]. Four. You and I, Mrs. Whichello. Where will you sit? [*Shuffling the cards vigorously.*]

MARY. Here.

[FELIX *puts the cards he is shuffling before* DICK, *who cuts to* MARY. MARY *deals.*]

DICK. You're sure you can keep me out of a law-suit, Galpin?

FELIX [*Vigorously shuffling the other cards*]. If I handle the case. "Never go to law" is the advice I always give my clients. And up to the present I've kept them out of it.

MARY. And I shan't have to apologize?

FELIX. Never!

CHESHER. How much are we playing for?

DICK. Five shillings a hundred?

MARY. Oh, · say ten. I'm thirsting for some-body's blood!

DICK [*Groans*]. You're going to draw mine if you don't take care!

MARY. Hold your tongue, Dick.

ELLA *enters from curtains and comes up to table.*

DICK. You'd better come round and see me in the morning.

FELIX. Right. What time?

DICK. Ten. No, I've got to play golf. I'm full up all day. [*To* MARY.] Why couldn't you keep your mouth shut?

MARY. Keep your cards up.

ELLA. What's the matter?

DICK. Mary is going to let me in for a lawsuit with the Bodsworths.

ELLA. What fun!

MARY. No trumps!

Quick curtain.

[49]

ACT II

Six weeks pass between Acts I and II.

ACT II

SCENE: *The same.   About four o'clock on an afternoon in late February.   The curtains are closely drawn, shutting out the further room.   A bright fire is burning.*

Discover: FELIX *with four or five dictionaries on table in front of him; one is open, and he is bending over it.*

Enter DAKIN, *showing in* ELLA *in pretty winter outdoor dress.   Exit* DAKIN.   FELIX *rises, takes* ELLA's *hand, kisses her in silence.*

FELIX.   You're a little late.   I hope Mrs. Whichello won't be long.   I've had to leave the office and there's only the boy.

ELLA.   Mary's coming on.   Dick and she are having another row.

FELIX.   Over the Bodsworth business?

ELLA.   Naturally.   There has been no other

[53]

business in our house since the night of your dinner. Dick and Mary argue and argue and argue. Felix, when we're married, we shan't be always arguing like that, shall we?

FELIX. Certainly not. I'll do all my arguing in Court.

ELLA. It would be so dreadful, if we got quarrelling, just like ordinary married people.

FELIX. How can they do it? How can they do it?

ELLA. And Mary is so perfectly right, isn't she?

FELIX. Perfectly right.

ELLA. She can't give a written apology?

FELIX. Out of the question.

ELLA. If the Bodsworths take it into Court, we shall win, shan't we?

FELIX. We've got to — somehow. This is my first important case, and I can't afford to lose it. Especially as I've just got the chance of another.

ELLA. Have you?

FELIX. Borrodaile was in my office this morning. He's inclined to fight the Church people over the new cemetery and crematorium.

ELLA. I hope he will. Did you encourage him?

[54]

FELIX. I said, "Never go to law. But," I said, "in this instance, I don't see how you can possibly lose."

ELLA. Yes, that's the way to put it.

FELIX. Oh, by the way — [*drawing a letter from his pocket and giving it to* ELLA] — my uncle has promised to tide me over another year.

ELLA. Isn't he a brick! [*Reading.*] "I am persuaded that a young man with your flexible convictions is bound to succeed."

FELIX. He's a good judge of character. Read on. He's called to a consultation at Barsfield, so he's dropping in on his way back to town.

ELLA. Oh, yes. [*Reading.*] "So I shall be with you a little after three."

FELIX. Things are looking up at last ——

ELLA. Yes, if you get the cemetery case — do you think you will?

FELIX. Well, Borrodaile is a stiff-necked old Radical. He hinted pretty strongly that he couldn't employ a Tory lawyer.

ELLA. Couldn't you — manage to drop being a Tory — just for the time?

FELIX. I've a jolly good mind to drop being a Tory altogether. Oh! I ought to have gone in for

[55]

politics at the start!   Look at my old chum, Harvey Betts ——

ELLA.   Yes.   Mary wants to talk to you about him ——

Enter DAKIN, *showing in* MARY.

DAKIN [*Announces*].   Mrs. Whichello.
   [*Exit* DAKIN.   MARY *is smartly dressed in winter clothes.*]

FELIX.   How d'ye do?

MARY [*Curtly*].   How d'ye do?   [*Barely shakes hands, and drops into a chair.*]   I do think my husband is the most stupid, obstinate man on earth!

FELIX.   Oh, not quite so bad as that, is he?

MARY [*Decisively*].   Now, Mr. Galpin, this affair of the Bodsworths must be brought to a head.

FELIX.   Well, it seems to be shaping that way.

MARY.   The question is whether you are on Dick's side or mine?

FELIX.   On yours — certainly on yours.

MARY.   Because Dick says you entirely agree with him that a lawsuit must be avoided.

FELIX.   Oh, no, oh, no   My advice is, "Never go to law if you can possibly avoid it."   But there are times when you can't possibly avoid it.

MARY. Well, Dick's coming on here directly ——

FELIX. I must talk to him.

MARY. I hope you will. Because I may tell you plainly that if you wish to be engaged to Ella, you will insist to my husband that it would be a fatal step for me to apologize.

FELIX. I'll put that strongly to him.

MARY. You'd better, if you wish to marry Ella.

ELLA. Oh, I couldn't think of giving him up! Could I, Felix?

MARY. My dear Ella, you couldn't possibly marry Mr. Galpin if he gets your sister into a horrible mess, and makes her cave in to that dreadful old impropriety.

ELLA. But Felix won't, will you?

FELIX. You may rely I shall do everything in my power to convince Mr. Whichello.

MARY. Very well. If you bring Dick round to our way of thinking, I'll take care he gives his consent to your marriage with Ella as soon as this has all blown over.

ELLA. There, Felix. You will stick to Mary, won't you?

FELIX. I will, like a leech.

MARY. Then, that's settled. Now, Ella, I want

[57]

to talk to Mr. Galpin. The motor's outside. You go on to Carrick and Green's, and get your dress tried on. I'll be there to try on mine as soon as you've finished. Send the motor back for me.

ELLA. All right. [*Going to door. To* FELIX.] Don't come down — no surrender! No apology! Down with the Bodsworths! Down with impropriety! [*Exit.*

MARY. Have you seen Mr. Tadman?

FELIX. Yes. He says the story is being repeated all over the town, and Lady Bodsworth is obliged to insist on the apology.

MARY. You told him I wouldn't sign?

FELIX. I said I would submit it to you, but I feared it would be useless. [*Draws a large blue envelope out of his pocket, takes out a blue paper and gives it to* MARY, *who reads it.*] Tadman is calling on Sir Thomas this afternoon for final instructions. He said he'd look in here on his way up.

MARY [*Having looked at the paper, gives a little shriek, reads a little further, gives a louder shriek*]. Sign this? Why doesn't she ask me to sweep her doorsteps? [*About to tear it up.*]

FELIX. No, don't tear it. I must show it to Whichello.

[58]

MARY. No, he might want me to sign it.

FELIX. Well, I must keep it for reference. [*She gives him the paper.*]

MARY. "Undertake not to repeat ——"! When she's going about telling everybody the most dreadful — there's no other word — lies about it. The account she gave to the Petburys when they lunched there! Never mind! I gave Lady Petbury my version. I kept her laughing for an hour.

FELIX. I wouldn't say anything about it while there's a lawsuit pending.

MARY. Not say anything about it? Oh, yes, I shall! Every day I think of something fresh!

FELIX. I hope you're careful to say nothing that isn't strictly accurate.

MARY. Accurate? You don't expect me to be accurate after the awful things she is saying about me?

FELIX. You must remember it will all be taken back to her.

MARY. Yes! That's exactly what I want. I thought of two perfectly fiendish additions yesterday ——

FELIX. You haven't used them, I trust?

MARY. Yes, I went round to Mrs. Bratwick and

told her. Mrs. Bratwick is her dearest friend, so
knew she'd go straight and tell the impropriety.

FELIX. You mustn't use that word ——

MARY. Oh, everybody calls her that now. She'
never be known as anything else. Now, how soo
shall we have a General Election?

FELIX. Within a few months — certainly withi
a year. What has that got to do with it?

MARY. Mr. Elkington's majority was only seven
teen. They say he'll lose the seat next time.

FELIX. Most likely, I should say.

MARY. Dick has always been a Tory, but they'r
having dreadful rows on the Town Council about th
new cemetery and the tramways. Dick is disguste
with them. I'm persuading him to turn Liberal.

FELIX. That wouldn't win us our lawsuit.

MARY. No, but — Mr. Harvey Betts, the Junio
Liberal Whip, is a great friend of yours?

FELIX. Yes, we're old Carthusians. Harvey is
big man now. I wish I'd gone in for politics!

MARY. Couldn't you invite Mr. Betts down for
week-end?

FELIX. Oh, yes. But how would that serve us

MARY. If Dick would only turn Liberal, and wi
the seat for them ——

FELIX. What then?

MARY. There was an old baronetcy in the Whichello family. It has been extinct for over a hundred
years ——

FELIX. They'd scarcely give Whichello a baronetcy for winning the Warkinstall seat.

MARY. No, not for merely winning the seat.
But — aren't there other ways?

FELIX. What do you mean?

MARY. Don't they give baronetcies and peerages to people who subscribe to the party funds?

FELIX. Yes — but they have to fork out pretty
heavily.

MARY. How much?

FELIX. Heaven only knows — and the party
leaders.

MARY. Couldn't you get Mr. Betts down and
find out from him how much?

FELIX. Oh, I daresay Harvey would come. But
to get a title you have to be deserving in other ways.

MARY. How deserving?

FELIX. Well, Bodsworth happened to be building a sanatorium, and it came in just handy for the
insurance Act.

MARY [*After a little thoughtful pause*]. Dick shall

[61]

give the town the new cemetery and crematorium [*Suddenly bursts into laughter.*] Ha! ha! ha!

FELIX. What's the matter?

MARY. Fancy Lady Bodsworth having to be cremated in our crematorium! Ha! ha! Or even only buried!

FELIX. At the rate we're going on, it will cost us a lot before we do get rid of her.

MARY. Never mind! It has got to be done!

FELIX. I don't know what we're going to let Whichello in for.

MARY. We're going to let him in for a baronetcy.

FELIX. Yes, but will he stand the racket?

MARY. He'll have to stand the racket. You aren't going to turn on his side, are you?

FELIX. No, but hadn't we better tot up before we go any further? Now this lawsuit — suppose it goes against us?

MARY. It wouldn't cost very much, would it?

FELIX. Can't say. Some hundreds at least. A good deal would depend upon the impression you make on the jury.

MARY. Oh, I think I can manage that. Lady Bodsworth will have to appear, too?

FELIX. Of course.

MARY. In that wig? Oh, we shall romp in!

FELIX. Yes, but the other side will want to know exactly what you meant by "impropriety."

MARY. Well, what did I?

FELIX. Well, what did you?

MARY. You said you'd look me up a meaning.

FELIX [*Going to the dictionaries*]. I asked McClintock to lend me his big etymological dictionary. He sent these in just before lunch.

Enter DAKIN, *showing in* CHESHER.

CHESHER. How are you, Felix?

FELIX. How are you?

CHESHER. Mrs. Whichello — delighted to meet you again! [*Shaking hands.*]

MARY. You're paying us another visit?

CHESHER. I've just looked in for an hour on my way back to town. Everything going well? I hope that little affair with the Bodsworths has quite blown over?

FELIX. Not quite. Mrs. Whichello and I were just talking it over.

CHESHER. Then I'm in the way. [*Preparing to go.*]

MARY. No, don't go. Perhaps you could help us.

[63]

CHESHER. Delighted. But how can I be of an use?

MARY. If you were on the jury, would you thin "impropriety" a very dreadful word?

CHESHER. Well, it depends upon the way it wa used — and who used it.

MARY. I used it. You remember that night Mr. Galpin's dinner party, and you remember ho Lady Bodsworth looked. Now, don't you think was quite justified? [CHESHER *does not answer* Under the circumstances?

CHESHER. Well, I shan't be on the jury.

MARY. No, but if you were? Tell me candidly

CHESHER. What was the exact phrase?

FELIX [*Quoting*]. "With her powdered cheek and her yellow hair, she looks like an impropriety.

MARY. Did I say that?

FELIX. Those were the exact words. [*Referrin to the blue paper.*]

MARY. Are you quite sure? I know I used th word "impropriety," but, if I remember rightly, didn't use it in any derogatory sense.

FELIX. Sir Thomas had the words taken dow that night. Mrs. Tadman will swear to them, an they are prepared to subpœna Miss Southwood.

MARY. Ella? Ella doesn't remember exactly hat I said, but she's quite sure I didn't mean any-ing horrid.

FELIX. Unfortunately Miss Southwood won't ave to decide what you meant. The other side aim that "impropriety" means a — a — a lady of certain class.

MARY. Oh, no! Oh, no! I didn't mean that.

FELIX. They will put it to the jury that you did,

MARY. Dr. Chesher, if you were on the jury, you ouldn't say that "impropriety" means — a — a — ould you?

CHESHER. Isn't it a useful variant for ——?

MARY. For what?

CHESHER. You know our English way. When e want to escape from a fact we escape from a ord. When the fact turns up again, we escape to nother word. In the end, we find we haven't abol-hed the fact. We have merely corrupted the nglish language.

MARY. I haven't corrupted the English language, ave I? We must have some word for a — that sort ' lady.

CHESHER. We had a good Bible and Shakespear-n word, but it was too painfully exact to be applied,

so we escaped to more pleasing substitutes. Th
early Victorian term was amiably descriptive, an
carried a mild reproof.

MARY. What was that?

CHESHER. About eighteen-forty it was custom
ary to speak of a "Fie! Fie!"

MARY. I never heard the word.

CHESHER. "Fille de joie" seems to be growin
daily more appropriate, judging from the appear
ances of some of our fashionable restaurants. Ther
are many other more or less suitable terms. Thos
who are curious in such lore may slake their thir:
for knowledge in Parminter's "Dictionary of Polit
Synonyms."

FELIX [*Has been busy over the dictionaries*]. W
haven't yet decided what Mrs. Whichello meant b
impropriety.

MARY. I meant — what do the dictionaries say
means?

FELIX [*Reading from a dictionary*]. "Impropriet;
the quality of being improper. An erroneous, or u
suitable expression, act," etc. [MARY *shakes her head*

FELIX [*Turning to another dictionary*]. "Impr
priety: that which is improper." Quotation fro
Jane Austen.

CHESHER. Surely not!

FELIX. "Elizabeth had never been blind to the improprieties of her father's behavior."

MARY. Well, I wasn't blind to the impropriety of Lady's Bodsworth's behavior. What else?

FELIX [*Reading from another dictionary*]. "Impropriety: indelicacy, unseemliness ——"

MARY [*Jumps at it*]. "Unseemliness!" That's what I meant! No jury would give heavy damages for "unseemliness."

FELIX. You can never tell what a jury will do.

MARY. Dr. Chesher, if you were on the jury ——

CHESHER. Ah, but I'm not.

MARY. But would you give heavy damages merely because I said that Lady Bodsworth's way of dressing her hair was unseemly?

CHESHER. Pardon me, was that exactly what you said?

MARY. Never mind what I said. That was what I meant. [CHESHER *shows surprise.*] Surely I must know what I meant. And if you were on the jury, and I told you that all I meant was that Lady Bodsworth's hair was unseemly, wouldn't you believe me?

CHESHER. I'm very much afraid I should.

[67]

MARY [*To* FELIX]. We'll stick to unseemliness!

Enter DAKIN.

DAKIN. Mr. Tadman is below, sir.

FELIX. I'll come down to him.

MARY. Couldn't he come up here?

FELIX [*To* DAKIN]. Show Mr. Tadman up.

DAKIN. Yes, sir.

CHESHER. Felix, I shall be going up by the five-thirty. I'll see you by and by. [*To* MARY.] If I can't be of any further use ——

MARY. You might stay and tell Mr. Tadman that if you were on the jury ——

CHESHER [*Shakes his head with a chuckle*]. Ah, but I'm not going to be.   [*Pops off.*

[*Exit* CHESHER, *leaving door open. A moment later is heard to say,* "How d'ye do?" TAD-MAN'S *voice responds,* "How d'ye do, Doctor?"]

FELIX [*To* MARY]. Now, you will be careful with Tadman — don't repeat "impropriety."

MARY. No — "unseemliness."

FELIX. We might try a bit of bluff ——

MARY. Yes. How?

[68]

FELIX. Shush!

Enter DAKIN, *announcing* TADMAN. *Enter* TADMAN.
Exit DAKIN.

TADMAN. How d'ye do, Mrs. Whichello?

MARY. How d'ye do?

TADMAN. How do again, Galpin?

FELIX. Take a seat, won't you?

TADMAN [*Sitting*]. I can't stay. Sir Thomas is expecting me. I hope Mrs. Whichello consents to an apology?

FELIX [*Firmly*]. I don't think so, eh, Mrs. Whichello?

MARY. Certainly not.

TADMAN. Then we must take it into Court?

FELIX. I suppose Sir Thomas and Lady Bodsworth fully realize what that means?

TADMAN. Pretty heavy damages, I should say.

FELIX. What for? Mrs. Whichello inadvertently makes a playful little comment on Lady Bodsworth ——

TADMAN. Playful little comment!

FELIX. For which she expresses her deep regret. Lady Bodsworth refuses to accept our apologies, and insists on bringing it before a jury. Well, now,

Tadman, are you really going to allow Lady Bodsworth to offer her hair and complexion to the contemplation of a jury? [MARY *gives a little chuckle.*] And so justify Mrs. Whichello's playful little comment?

TADMAN. I suppose Mrs. Whichello knows the implied meaning of impropriety?

MARY. Yes, it means "unseemliness."

[TADMAN *gives a derisive little grunt.*]

It says so in the dictionary.

[TADMAN *again gives a little grunt.*]

FELIX. Mrs. Whichello will be delighted to explain to the jury exactly what she meant.

[TADMAN *again gives a little grunt.*]

MARY. I'm longing to go into the box — simply longing.

FELIX. Our counsel will be instructed to treat the whole matter as a farce. He may perhaps suggest to Mrs. Whichello a few playful variations on the original theme.

TADMAN. That will increase our chance of getting heavy damages.

FELIX. Heavy damages? Why, you know, Tadman, this is just the sort of case that a judge and jury look upon as a day's outing. Suppose Sparling gets hold of it! Heavy damages? You'll get a farthing!

And the next day all the papers will have chaffing articles on Lady Bodsworth's complexion, and she'll be known all over the country as an impropriety — whatever that may mean. Is that what Sir Thomas wants? Just as he's going up to get his title! You know best.

TADMAN [*Rising*]. Then Mrs. Whichello declines to sign the apology?

MARY. Positively!

TADMAN. I'll tell Sir Thomas your decision.

Enter DAKIN, *announcing* MR. WHICHELLO. *Enter*
    DICK. *Exit* DAKIN. DICK *is evidently in a ruffled
    temper.*

DICK [*Curtly*]. How d'ye do, Galpin? Ah, Tadman, I'm very glad to find you here. [MARY *makes signs to* DICK *to be quiet. He takes no notice.*] Now, Tadman, this confounded thing has gone far enough. Can't we get it settled?

        [MARY *gives a little shriek and shows intense
            annoyance.*]

TADMAN. Nothing would please us better. I have handed Mr. Galpin a form of apology.

MARY [*Decisively*]. Which I shall not sign.

DICK [*Impatiently*]. Tsh! Tsh! Tsh!

[71]

[FELIX *takes the form of apology from his pocket
and gives it to* DICK. MARY *makes signs to*
FELIX *while* DICK *reads the apology.*]

DICK [*Having read it*]. Yes — well, this is a bit
stiff ——

MARY. Stiff! It's an insult, isn't it, Mr. Galpin?

DICK [*Impatiently*]. Tsh! Tsh! Tsh! [*To* TAD-
MAN.] I've just seen Monkhouse, and he tells
me that as an old friend of us both, he has got Sir
Thomas to promise to meet me and talk this over
amicably.

MARY. Mr. Galpin and I have decided upon a
course of action ——

DICK. Have you? Well, I have decided upon a
course of action.

[MARY *in despair sits down, looks very obstinate,
taps the ground impatiently with her feet,
exchanges glances with* FELIX, *and makes
contemptuous gestures as* DICK *proceeds.*]

DICK. Now, Tadman, will you tell Sir Thomas that
I shall be pleased to talk this over in a friendly way?

TADMAN. Certainly. When and where?

DICK. This is neutral ground. If he wouldn't
mind stepping round ——

TADMAN. I'll suggest that to Sir Thomas.

DICK. And if he'll meet me over the apology, I'll meet him over the tramways and the cemetery.

MARY. We must have a cemetery. And a crematorium.

DICK. Tsh! Tsh! Tsh! Bring him along. Galpin, I hope I may rely on you to help me arrange this with Sir Thomas.

FELIX. Certainly. [*Rings bell.*]

TADMAN [*Takes up his hat and is going*]. I've no doubt Sir Thomas will be ready to listen to any proposal ——

MARY. I daresay he will! Rather than allow Lady Bodsworth to go into the witness box with that very unseemly hair and complexion!

DICK [*Angrily*]. Mary!

[DAKIN *appears at door.*]

FELIX. The door, Dakin.

TADMAN [*To* DICK]. I'll take your message to Sir Thomas. [*Exit* TADMAN, *followed by* DAKIN.

MARY. Well, my dear Dick, of all the silly, footling, stupid, absurd things you've done in your life, this caps everything!

DICK. How so?

MARY. Just as Mr. Galpin and I had planned it all, you must needs come in and spoil everything!

[73]

DICK. Spoil what?

MARY. We'd frightened Mr. Tadman into a blue funk. The Bodsworths wouldn't have dared to come into Court! You'd have gone into Parliament. The old baronetcy would have been revived — and then you blunder in, and give it all away! [*Throws up her arms in despair, and walks about desperately.*]

DICK. Old baronetcy? Nonsense! The Kellaton Whichellos were no connection of my family.

MARY. They must have been! Mr. Galpin, will you please trace out my husband's relationship to the Kellaton Whichellos?

DICK [*Turns round on* FELIX]. Galpin, I hope you're no party to this silly scheme of my wife's?

MARY. Yes. Mr. Galpin was saying ten minutes ago, "if Whichello had any pluck he'd rouse himself and fight, and we could sweep the floor with the Bodsworths."

DICK. Galpin, you didn't say that?

FELIX. Not precisely in those words. But I do think Mrs. Whichello's plan is worth your consideration. If it could be carried out — mind you, I don't say that it could, but if it could, — it would place you in the leading position in Warkinstall.

MARY. Of course it would, and what are you

[74]

now? What am I? You say yourself that Sir Thomas is sitting on you on the Town Council! He's sitting on everybody! If you don't take care, my dear Dick, you'll very soon be a cipher in Warkinstall!

DICK. That's all very well — but what can I do?

MARY. Rouse yourself! As Mr. Galpin says, "Fight him!" Fight him over the tramways! Fight him over the cemetery! Fight him over everything! Put up for Parliament ——

DICK. Put up for Parliament — as a Liberal?

MARY. Why not? You don't believe in food taxes.

DICK. No, but I'm a staunch Tariff Reformer. That is, if the leather trade is properly considered.

MARY. You can't be a Tariff Reformer if you've read that little pamphlet I gave you. It proves that under Tariff Reform we shall all be starving in six months. It quite convinced me.

DICK. But you canvassed for Elkington and Tariff Reform at the last election!

MARY. Well, next election I'm going to canvass for you, and no food taxes. You surely don't mean to let the Bodsworths ride roughshod over us for the

[75]

rest of our lives? Do have the courage of your convictions!

DICK. But I can't rat from the party ——

MARY. It isn't ratting. It's getting broader, more enlightened ideas, isn't it, Mr. Galpin?

FELIX. After all, Whichello, it's only looking at things from a Liberal point of view instead of a Conservative. That's all it amounts to.

DICK. But I shall have to give up my Club, and all my friends. It's the only place in the town where I can get a decent game of billiards. By Jove, yes, and I shall have to hobnob with Borrodaile and all the Dissenting set.

MARY. Well, they're very nice — when you get to know them. And you needn't know them very much.

DICK. And what's it going to cost? Lawsuit, baronetcy, Parliament — I should have to be in London three parts of my time — I should never get a round of golf —— No, I'm hanged if I do!

MARY. Very well, my dear Dick. Then Warkinstall will be simply impossible for me.

DICK [*After further deep reflection, says more emphatically*]. No, I'm hanged if I do! No! We haven't long to live in this world! Do let us be happy, do let us be comfortable while we are here.

MARY. Comfortable! Going in second to Lady Bodsworth all my life! You don't call that being comfortable?

Enter DAKIN.

DAKIN [*To* MARY]. Please, ma'am, Carrick and Green have rung up to ask if you wish to try on your dress before the light goes.

MARY. I'll come at once. [*Exit* DAKIN.] So if that's your decision, Dick, we had better let our house here, and move up to London.

DICK. What for?

MARY. I cannot live in a town where I am constantly trampled under foot by a yellow-haired — unseemliness.

DICK. Nonsense! You run along and try on your dress.

MARY. Mr. Galpin, I shan't be long. Please see that nothing is settled in my absence. [*He is accompanying her.*] No — please stay and try to rouse my husband to a sense of his duty to himself. [*Exit.*

DICK [*Turns round on* FELIX]. Now, Galpin, what's the meaning of this?

[77]

FELIX.   Meaning of what?

DICK.   I thought you were on my side.

FELIX.   So I am! So I am!

DICK.   But Mrs. Whichello says you are advising her it will have to go into Court.

FELIX.   No! No! Not if we can possibly keep it out.

DICK.   I'm quite determined I'll keep it out.

FELIX.   Quite right! "Never go to law." But there are times in every man's life when he feels that ——

DICK.   Yes.   Well, this is one of the times in my life when I don't feel like that at all.

FELIX.   When he feels that he owes it to his own dignity to ——

DICK.   I don't feel I owe a ha'penny to my own dignity.   And I'll take jolly good care I don't owe a thousand pounds or two to you lawyers — if I can help it.

FELIX.   I'm ready to carry out your instructions. At the same time, I may point out to you one or two facts ——

DICK.   Yes.   Well, let me point out to you one or two facts.   The first fact is, I'm Miss Southwood's guardian.   The second fact is, I've got control of her money till she's twenty-five. The third fact, I've made up my mind I won't have a lawsuit with the Bodsworths. [*Emphasizing his words by bringing his fist on the table.*]

FELIX. Oh, I'm quite with you — quite.

DICK. Now you wish to be engaged to Miss Southwood, don't you?

FELIX. With your consent.

DICK. Very well. Then I'll give you a very straight tip. You get me out of this mess with the Bodsworths, and persuade my wife to give up this silly nonsense of going into Parliament, and getting a baronetcy, and when you propose for Miss Southwood I shall most likely say, "Yes." What do you say?

FELIX. Oh, certainly, certainly.

DICK. I may rely on you?

FELIX. Absolutely. [*Looks very uncomfortable.*]

DICK. That's all right then. I shall leave Mrs. Whichello entirely in your hands. [FELIX's *face drops and grows longer and longer as* DICK *proceeds.*] My wife is the dearest little woman in the world. But when once she gets an idea in her head, she is the most aggravating, unreasonable, won't-let-you-have-any-peace-till-she-gets-it creature that ever breathed.

FELIX. She is rather persistent.

DICK. Good Lord, yes! You've no idea what my life has been the last six weeks. I haven't had a moment's peace. That's why I think it will be better for you to take her in hand.

FELIX [*Getting more uncomfortable*]. I very much question the wisdom of my interfering.

DICK. Oh, there won't be any interfering. I shall simply stand aside, and give you carte blanche to bring her round to her senses. The fact is, Galpin, I know jolly well that if she keeps on at me I shall find myself let in for the lawsuit, and the baronetcy and all the rest of it, before I know where I am. That's why I want you to come in as a buffer.

FELIX. It's rather a ticklish thing to come in between man and wife ——

DICK. So it is, as a rule. But this is just one of those cases where a third party can step in and ease off the friction.

FELIX. Well, I'll do my best, but ——

DICK. That's a dear, good chap. I knew you would. I'm much obliged to you. You pull this off and then come and ask me for Ella. [*Offers his hand shakes hands with* FELIX *cordially*.] I feel a load is off my mind. [*Looks at his watch*.] She'll be an hour

iddling over her dress. Now let's look alive and fix
his up with Bodsworth and Tadman while she's out
of the way.

MARY *enters.*

DICK. Hillo! Hillo! I thought you were trying
on your dress ——

MARY. I was so much upset I couldn't fix my
mind on it. It flashed upon me that if I wasn't
here, you would simply lie down and ask Sir Thomas
to walk over you.

DICK [*Getting angry*]. I'm not going to let Bodsworth or any other man walk over me.

MARY. Yes, you will, my dear Dick, if I'm not
here.

DICK. You toddle back again to Carrick and
Green's and try on your dress.

[MARY *replies by seating herself calmly.* DICK
looks in despair at FELIX, *and makes a mute
appeal for help.*]

FELIX [*After a little hesitation*]. Perhaps you and
might run round to Sir Thomas.

DICK. Yes —— [*Preparing to go.*]

MARY. He's here. I saw his motor coming
round the corner.

Enter DAKIN.

DAKIN. Sir Thomas and Mr. Tadman are in the morning-room, sir. Shall I show them up?

DICK. We'll go down to them, Galpin—— [*Moving toward door*.]

MARY [*Rising*]. Yes.

DICK. No, you'd better stay here — eh, Galpin?

FELIX [*To* MARY]. Perhaps you'd better let us open up the question. We'll refer everything to you as we go along.

MARY [*Firmly*]. No, Mr. Galpin. You know Dick's good nature. He's no match for a strong determined man like Sir Thomas.

DICK. I'm no match for Bodsworth?

MARY. No, my dear Dick, you know you aren't. He'll make you say and do just whatever he pleases.

DICK. Oh, will he? We shall see. [*To* DAKIN.] Please show Sir Thomas and Mr. Tadman up.

DICK. No, Dakin—— [*Looks appealingly at* FELIX.]

FELIX [*To* DAKIN, *who is going*]. One moment Dakin. [*To* MARY.] Suppose you and I just step into the next room. [*With a sly, persuading look and half-wink at her, unseen by* DICK.] We shall then b

[82]

able to follow the course of the negotiations —— [*With another sly, persuading look and half-wink, coaxing her off.*]

MARY [*Moving a reluctant step toward curtains*]. I don't like listening.

FELIX. No, neither do I, but — [*another look and half-wink*] — we can better keep an eye on the situation. [*With another look and wink.* MARY *goes up to curtains and passes through reluctantly.*]

FELIX [*To* DAKIN]. Show Sir Thomas and Mr. Tadman up. Don't mention that Mrs. Whichello is here. [*Exit* DAKIN.

DICK [*In a whisper to* FELIX]. Keep her quiet!

[FELIX *throws* DICK *a confident glance of assurance, and a half-wink, goes through curtains. Left alone,* DICK *shakes his head dubiously, as if dissatisfied with the situation, goes up to curtains, calls out to* MARY.]

DICK. Now, Mary, please let me have a quiet five minutes with Bodsworth, and don't interrupt.

MARY [*Within*]. All right, I'll look out of the window.

DICK [*Suspicious*]. Galpin, just see that we're not disturbed, there's a good fellow. [*He shakes his head again, very doubtfully.*]

[83]

Enter DAKIN, *showing in* SIR THOMAS *and*
MR. TADMAN. *Exit* DAKIN.

DICK [*Goes to* SIR THOMAS *very cordially, offers his hand*]. Ah, Sir Thomas, I'm delighted to meet you—— [SIR THOMAS, *stolid and rather cold, shakes hands.*] Our old friend Monkhouse wants us to make this up. He says you are quite willing.

SIR T. I'm ready to discuss the matter. Mr. Galpin is not here?

DICK [*Glancing nervously round at curtains*]. I've asked him to let you and me have a quiet five minutes together. [*Drawing* SIR THOMAS *away from the curtains and speaking in a low voice.*] Now, you and I are sensible men, Bodsworth, aren't we?

SIR T. I have always prided myself upon my good sense, and the clear view I take of things.

DICK. And I hope I'm not an utter ass. Well, let us start from that platform, and work from that.

TADMAN. An excellent platform! Two sensible men! Work from that!

DICK [*Glancing nervously at curtains; drawing* SIR THOMAS *further away; dropping his voice still lower*]. Now, between ourselves, old friend, if our wives choose to quarrel, there's no reason that you and I

[84]

should be fools enough to follow suit, and make ourselves the laughing-stock of the town.

Sir T. I am not accustomed to regard myself as a
laughing-stock.

Dick. No! No! [*Dropping his voice again, always with a nervous eye on the curtains.*] But folks
are laughing at us, aren't they, Tadman?

Tadman. They are taking that view of it.

Dick. I've never been so much chaffed in my life.
And they'll laugh more if we're fools enough to go
to law.

Sir T. I am quite prepared to arrange it.

Dick. Very well. Then — [*dropping his voice*]—
we agree to settle it amicably.

Sir T. On a satisfactory basis.

Dick. Of course, on a satisfactory basis. [*Whis-
pering.*] The great thing is, we don't go to law. Let's
shake hands on that. [*Offering hand; they shake
hands,* Dick *very cordially.*]

Tadman. That's what I advised on the night —
arrange it amicably.

Dick. So you did, Tadman. Well, we have arranged it amicably. Now — [*dropping his voice to a
coaxing whisper and drawing them toward him*] —
let's all meet at the Club in an hour's time, and settle

the details over a bottle of champagne. I'll bring Galpin on.

SIR T. I have promised Lady Bodsworth that no step shall be taken without her knowledge.

DICK [*Is upset*]. Oh! [*Dropping his voice.*] I don't think that's wise! [*Coaxing.*] Hadn't we better fix it up at the Club, and tell our wives afterwards? You can send Tadman on to tell Lady Bodsworth, and I'll send Galpin on to tell Mrs. Whichello. And you and I can stay on at the Club, and have a little friendly dinner together, eh?

SIR T. [*Firmly*]. I have given my pledge to Lady Bodsworth to settle nothing without her. She is waiting in the motor outside. I had better bring her up —— [*Making a little movement toward door.*]

DICK. I don't think I would! [*Coming up very cautiously to* SIR T., *speaking in a nervous whisper.*] Can't we all pop down to the Club ——

SIR T. [*Getting very suspicious, speaks loudly*]. Pop down to the Club? Why should we pop down to the Club? We are doing nothing to be ashamed of, I hope?

DICK. No, no ——

SIR T. Then why do you speak in whispers?

Don't you wish everything to be open and above-board?

DICK. Oh, yes, oh, yes ——

SIR T. Then as Lady Bodsworth is the insulted party ——

DICK. Oh, not insulted ——

SIR T. Not insulted? She is designated as an "impropriety," and she is not insulted?

DICK. Well, we needn't go into that just now——

SIR T. But that is precisely what we must go into. And if you wish to settle it amicably ——

DICK. I do, I do. But I do think that Lady Bodsworth's presence — eh, Tadman?

TADMAN. I don't see how we can arrive at any understanding without Lady Bodsworth's sanction.

SIR T. Certainly not. Nor shall I be any party to "popping into the Club," or any underhand negotiations whatever. Lady Bodsworth and I are willing to discuss the matter — without prejudice ——

TADMAN [*To* DICK]. You won't get a better chance to settle, Whichello.

SIR T. Then with Galpin's permission I will bring her up. Where is Galpin?

DICK. He'll be here directly. He popped into the next room at my request.

Sir T. [*Growing more suspicious*]. "Popped into the next room"? I don't like all this "popping" into next rooms, and "popping" into Clubs. Galpin had better be present if we are to come to a settlement. I'll fetch Lady Bodsworth. [*Exit.*

Dick [*Approaches* Tadman *in a cautious whisper*]. I got Galpin to take my wife into the next room —— [*Indicating curtains.*]

Tadman. There?

Dick. Yes. She's better out of the way. Now, Tadman, you're an old friend ——

Tadman. Certainly.

Dick [*Glancing nervously round at curtains*]. Well, let's look alive and fix this up amicably. You'll help me, won't you?

Tadman. Certainly.

Dick. Thanks. And if Galpin can only manage to keep her quiet for ten minutes ——

[*The curtains are moved aside, and* Felix *is seen to be restraining* Mary *from coming in.*]

Felix. We can keep an eye on the situation in here.

Mary [*Entering in spite of him*]. I prefer to keep an eye on the situation in here. [*Looks at* Dick *for two or three moments with an air of benevolent con-*

tempt and a little shrug.] Well, my dear Dick, so you've bungled it again!

DICK [*Getting angry*]. Bungled it! Oh, no, I haven't! I'm going to settle this amicably! [*Tapping the table emphatically with each word.*] D'ye see? Whether you like it or whether you don't, I'm going to settle it amicably! [*Again tapping the table.*]

MARY [*Serene*]. Very well, my dear Dick, settle it amicably.

DICK. I'm going to! [*With an emphatic nod of the head.*]

LADY BODSWORTH *enters, followed by* SIR THOMAS. *She has discarded her light wig, and her hair is now plainly brushed, of a dark-brown color, with a suspicion of being dyed. Her complexion is not made up, and is rather pale and pasty. The result is a startling change in her appearance.* DICK *has a little shock, and turns away to recover himself.* FELIX *has also a shock which he conceals as quickly as possible.* MARY *has a gaspy little chuckle, and turns to* FELIX, *who admonishes her into silence by a warning look.* MARY *immediately controls herself into preternatural gravity, but every now and then*

[89]

steals a sly look at FELIX *and nudges him very slightly with her elbow to look at* LADY BODSWORTH.

FELIX [*Offering hand*]. How d'ye do, Lady Bodsworth? [LADY BODSWORTH *takes his hand coldly*.] Do please be seated.

[LADY BODSWORTH *remains standing*.]

DICK. How d'ye do, Lady Bodsworth?

LADY B. [*Very self-conscious, preserving a stern dignity*]. I am quite well, I thank you.

DICK. Sir Thomas and I have made up our minds as old friends to settle this amicably.

LADY B. Of course, if you wish to apologize. [*Looking at* MARY.] I was not aware, when I came up, that I should be called upon to meet ——

MARY [*Looking at her, nods and speaks very sweetly*]. How d'ye do? You'll pardon me for not recognizing you at first, now that you're — [*looking at her*] — now that you're not — not so blond as you were.

[LADY BODSWORTH *gathers herself up with wrathful dignity and looks at* SIR THOMAS.]

SIR T. Whichello, if you wish to settle this amicably, you had better request Mrs. Whichello not to make any further remarks.

DICK. Ye-es. [*Looks imploringly at* MARY, *who*

[90]

is demure and determined — looks at TADMAN *and* FELIX *for support.*] Hadn't we better pop down — adjourn to the Club?

LADY B. I think as I have been insulted, I have a right to be present. [*Looks at* SIR THOMAS.]

SIR T. Certainly. Now, Whichello, Tadman and I are ready to listen to what you propose.

MARY. One moment, Sir Thomas. Something has just occurred to me — I should like to consult Mr. Galpin — please excuse me —— [*She draws* FELIX *aside, and is seen to be arguing a point; he shakes his head and demurs; she urges the point more strongly — he still endeavors to quiet her.* DICK *shows great irritation, and makes signs to her and* FELIX.]

MARY [*To* FELIX]. Yes! Yes! [*To* SIR T.] Please excuse us a moment. It's most important. [*To* FELIX.] Mr. Galpin, please ask Sir Thomas ——

FELIX. We needn't raise that question at present ——

MARY. Yes. Sir Thomas and Lady Bodsworth have a right to know ——

DICK [*Very much irritated*]. Galpin, don't let's mess about with any trumpery details. Let's get on to the main point, and settle it.

MARY. My dear Dick, this is the main point. Mr. Galpin, please explain to Sir Thomas ——

> [FELIX *again tries to dissuade her in dumb show.*]

SIR T. Now, Galpin, my time is precious. What is this point that Mrs. Whichello has raised?

FELIX [*Doesn't like the job*]. Mrs. Whichello says that if this case should unfortunately come into court — which we hope may be avoided — would Lady Bodsworth appear before the jury as she is now, or as she appeared on the night ——

> [LADY BODSWORTH *utters an indignant exclamation and looks at* SIR THOMAS.]

MARY. It wouldn't be fair not to give the jury an opportunity of judging ——

SIR T. [*Expands and explodes*]. Really — upon my word — I have never — Tadman, it's useless for us to remain any longer. Fanny! [*Prepares to go.*]

DICK [*Stopping him*]. No, Bodsworth, no! There's no need to get in a temper! You and I are sensible men! Let's talk it over quietly, as sensible men! Tadman, explain to Sir Thomas —— [*He urges* TADMAN *to mollify* SIR THOMAS. TADMAN *goes to* SIR THOMAS *and* LADY BODSWORTH, *and is seen to be soothing them.* DICK *goes to* FELIX *and* MARY, *and*

is seen to be arguing with MARY, *and begging her to
keep quiet. The two groups hold a little conference
apart from each other, and are seen to be talking it over.*]

TADMAN. Now, Whichello, Sir Thomas will hear
what you propose ——

SIR T. Without prejudice.

DICK. Well, first of all, I should be disposed to
give in to Sir Thomas over the tramways ——

SIR T. A very sensible determination.

DICK [*Irritated by* SIR T.'s *tone*]. You think so?
Well, I don't. Still, to avoid a row here, and a row
on the Council ——

SIR T. There need be no row if you stick to your
principles, Whichello, instead of playing into the
hands of the Liberal Party.

DICK [*Getting a little angry*]. Playing into the
hands of the Liberal Party?

SIR T. As you have been doing for the last six
months.

DICK. Good heavens! The town wants the tramways badly enough ——

TADMAN. Better leave that question, Whichello.
You wish to settle this matter amicably.

DICK [*Grudgingly*]. Well, I'll give in over the
tramways. And I'll give in over the cemetery and

[93]

the crematorium. And I call that a very handsome offer. Especially as the old churchyard is only a quarter of a mile above my factory, and a precious damp hole into the bargain.

SIR T. I must ask you not to speak disrespectfully of the hallowed spot where I intend to be buried.

MARY. Dick, you ought not to object to Sir Thomas getting buried where he likes.

DICK [*Turns round on her savagely*]. Will you please keep quiet. He may get buried whenever and wherever he pleases — for all I care. It's a mouldy, unwholesome bog, and it ought to be shut up. But rather than keep on having these perpetual rows over it, I'm willing to drop the new cemetery.

MARY. May I ask a question?

DICK [*Fiercely*]. No! For heaven's sake be quiet for five minutes, and let's get this settled.

MARY. But, my dear Dick, if we don't have a new cemetery, where are all the patients from Sir Thomas's sanatorium to be buried?

[SIR THOMAS *and* LADY BODSWORTH *show great anger.* TADMAN *quiets them down.*]

DICK [*Has turned fiercely on* MARY]. Will you please hold your tongue? You've got me into this

[94]

confounded muddle, and now you — [*sees* FELIX, *who has been standing quiet and impassive, turns savagely on him*] — Galpin, are you acting for me in this matter, or are you not?

FELIX. Yes ——

DICK. Well, what are you standing there for? Why on earth don't you back me up, and help me get this settled?

FELIX. If you'll give me your instructions ——

DICK. I have given you my instructions. Good heavens! If you're going to act for me, act for me, and don't stand there with your hands in your pockets! Act for me!

FELIX. Tadman, Mr. Whichello has made very liberal concessions over the tramways and the cemetery. I hope Sir Thomas considers them satisfactory.

SIR T. Quite satisfactory, so far as they go.

[DICK *gives an unconciliatory growl.*]

FELIX. In return for these concessions, Mr. Whichello expects certain concessions on your side — which he will now formulate. [*Looking at* DICK.]

TADMAN. Now, Whichello ——

DICK. Well, of course you'll agree to drop the lawsuit, and draw in over the apology; and I think Sir Thomas might let us have the slope under the sanatorium grounds for the golf club — at a valuation.

SIR T. Quite impossible. I consider that Englishmen waste far too much time on golf ——

DICK. Oh, you do? I suppose I'm the best judge of how I waste my time.

SIR T. Certainly. But if you were more often in your place on the Town Council, supporting me ——

DICK. Supporting you?

SIR T. Instead of playing into the hands of the Liberal Party when you do come ——

DICK [*Thoroughly roused*]. When I do come I'm going to vote for what I think right and proper, and I'm going to support just whom I jolly well please

[*Walking about, comes toward* MARY.

MARY [*In a low tone to* DICK]. He's walking over you!

DICK. Support you? Good Lord, you walk about like a little tin god, and you think you've got the town in your pocket! Support you? I'll let you see that you're not going to boss everybody and everything any longer! Warkinstall doesn't belong to you, does it? Support you? I'm going to support the tramways, and I'm going to support the new cemetery; so if you mean to be buried in that hole you'll have to look sharp about it, or we shall cremate you before you know you're dead!

SIR T. Very well. At the next meeting of the Conservative Association, I shall move that you are called upon to explain your action, or resign.

DICK. Resign? I do resign! I have resigned! Play into the hands of the Liberal Party? By Jove, I will! Galpin, will you see Borrodaile and the rest of them on my behalf, and say that if they consider me a suitable candidate, I shall be pleased to fight the town at the next election on Liberal principles! And a jolly stiff fight I shall put up, I assure you!

SIR T. Tadman, we needn't wait any longer — Fanny!

LADY B. There's nothing been said about the apology.

SIR T. We shall not accept an apology. Tadman, you will issue the writ at once. My wife an impropriety? We will see what a British jury says to that!

DICK [*Fiercely*]. We will see!

MARY [*Serenely*]. We will see!

SIR T. Good afternoon, Galpin. [*Bows to* MARY.]

FELIX. Good afternoon, Sir Thomas. [*Rings bell.*]

TADMAN. Good day, Galpin. Good day, Whichello. [DICK *nods curtly*.] Good afternoon, Mrs. Whichello.

MARY. Oh, Mr. Tadman, one moment. [*Appeals to* FELIX.] Mr. Galpin, we shall have a right to demand that the jury see the original coiffure —— [*Glancing at* LADY BODSWORTH, *who utters a little shriek, and makes a hurried exit.* SIR THOMAS *glares at* MARY, *and exits after* LADY BODSWORTH.]

FELIX. Certainly; I'm afraid, Tadman, our counsel will have to press Lady Bodsworth to oblige us on that point.

TADMAN. Oh, very well. Good day. [*Exit.*
[DICK *has seated himself, and has grown much calmer*.]

MARY [*Enthusiastically*]. Well, my dear Dick, I do congratulate you! [*Kissing him heartily*.] You've come to your senses at last!

DICK. Oh, I'm in for it now.

MARY. Yes. [*Excitedly*.] Now, we mustn't waste any time. Mr. Galpin, you'll be our election agent ——

FELIX. Delighted!

MARY. Write to Mr. Harvey Betts, and ask him to come down for the first week-end he can spare.

FELIX. Right.

MARY. Dick, you must join the Liberal Club ——

DICK. Yes, of course. I'm in for it now.

MARY. You'd better give them some weekly political addresses ——

DICK. Good Lord, what about?

FELIX. Don't you worry. I'll write out your addresses.

MARY. Who's the best counsel we can get for the lawsuit?

FELIX. Clapperton. He'll chaff Lady Bodsworth into a fit, and chaff the whole case out of Court.

MARY. Wire and retain him. [FELIX *sits down and hurriedly writes a telegram*.] Look cheerful, Dick!

DICK [*Getting very gloomy*]. Oh, I'm in for it now, and I'm going to see it through.

MARY. Of course you are. Ella shall drop in on Mrs. Bratwick, and mention that we're determined to have Lady Bodsworth in full fig at the trial. Mrs. Bratwick will take it to the impropriety, and then—— What's the matter, Dick?

DICK. Nothing—nothing. I'm thinking it over.

MARY. Well, look cheerful.

51074

FELIX [*Having written telegram*]. Yes, buck up, Whichello — we'll see you through.

DICK. Oh, I'm in for it now — and I'm not going to draw back.

MARY. Draw back?

DICK. I say I shan't.

MARY. I should think not! [*Having glanced at telegram which* FELIX *has held out before her.*] Yes — send it off at once. [FELIX *rings bell.*] And please hunt up all about Dick's pedigree and his claims to the Whichello baronetcy.

DICK. Baronetcy?

MARY. Yes. Look cheerful! Look cheerful! Look cheerful, Sir Richard!

Curtain

ACT III

Three weeks pass between Acts II and III

ACT III

SCENE: *The Same. About ten in the morning. The room much as in the last act.*

Discover FELIX *and* HARVEY BETTS, *each with a local paper in his hand.* HARVEY BETTS *is an alert, smart, youthful-looking aristocrat of thirty-five, with very bright, easy-going manners, and dressed in the very latest fashion.*

FELIX. Hillo, Harvey — they're tickling you — [*Reads from his paper.*] "Great interest attaches to the visit to our ancient borough of Mr. Harvey Betts, the brilliant young statesman, who has recently been appointed one of the whips of the Liberal Party. His presence amongst us sets the Government seal of approval upon our esteemed fellow-townsman, Mr. Richard Wichello, as Liberal Candidate at the next general election." What does the Tory rag say?

BETTS [*Reading*]. "The desperate straits to which

the Liberal Party is reduced in Warkinstall may be inferred from the fact that the blustering and blundering ratters, Whichello and Galpin — [*digging* FELIX] — the blustering and blundering ratters — have been obliged to summon to their aid the preposterous dandy who has recently been pichforked on to the Treasury Bench as Junior Whip. We shall see what the hard-headed, sturdy, common-sense workingmen of Warkinstall have to say to this egregious 'nut' without any kernel."

FELIX [*Reading*]. "The chairman, Mr. Bloxam Borrodaile, opened the meeting with a magnificent display of Boanerges eloquence which somewhat overshadowed the cautious and modest oratorical effort made by Mr. Whichello. Mr. Harvey Betts then followed with a lively attack upon the whole Tory position, which was left a crumbled mass of ruins. No less damaging was the vigorous onslaught made by Mr. Felix Galpin, who is rapidly becoming one of the rising hopes of the Liberal Party in Warkinstall. But the loudest cheers of the evening were reserved for our own Mary, as all true Liberals delight to call her. In a few terse and witty remarks she indicated some local Tory leaders, who would have the first claim to be accommodated in the new cemetery and crematorium which Mr. Whichello is presenting to the town."

BETTS [*Reading*]. "After the pitiable exhibition of his muddle-headed views which the turncoat Whichello made last evening, every self-respecting Conservative must rejoice that this incapable and incoherent wobbler has left the honest party. Straightforward, clear-sighted patriots will no longer have occasion to blush for this maundering renegade." I say, old man, you wrote me Whichello was a jolly good candidate.

FELIX. So he is. He has got six hundred workmen. What's the matter with him?

BETTS. He's the rankest duffer of a mugwump I ever met. He's shaky on Free Trade; he's shaky on Home Rule; he's shaky on Universal Suffrage; he's shaky on the whole bally bag of tricks.

FELIX. He has just ratted from the Tories, you know.

BETTS. Well, when a man rats, let him rat, and make no bones about it. Now I call you a good ratter.

FELIX. No mistake about me, eh? Rising hope of the Warkinstall Liberals — eh? [*Pointing enthusiastically to himself.*]

[105]

BETTS. You're all right. But what a ghastly mess Whichello made last night.

FELIX. He was pretty awful.

BETTS. I thought you had him in tow ——

FELIX. I wrote out his speech and coached him all yesterday afternoon. Then he never spoke a word of it.

BETTS. Tell you what, old man, we shall have to put some ginger into Whichello, or we shall come a howling cropper.

FELIX. Oh, he'll be right enough. You let Mrs. Whichello know where you want to find Whichello, and she'll take care he's on the spot.

BETTS. I wish we could run her. I'm in love with our own Mary. If it weren't for our own Mary I should drop Whichello like a hot potato. [*Dropping his voice.*] I say, old man, she keeps on digging at me for a baronetcy.

FELIX. You'll be able to manage it?

BETTS [*Shakes his head*]. It rests with the Chief. We've been chucking about a lot of peerages and baronetcies lately. What's this old Whichello baronetcy she keeps on bringing up? [**FELIX** *gives a shrug and grimace.*] Nothing in it — eh?

FELIX. Oh, there was one; and she says Whichello is the heir.

BETTS [*Cunningly.*] I suppose he'll plank down a pretty big lump for the Party war-chest?

FELIX. Oh, yes. He's pretty warm.

BETTS. The question is, how much will he stand? I must have a chat with him.

FELIX. I wouldn't. Take my tip. Settle the tariff with her, and leave her to bring Whichello to the scratch. [*With a little wink at* BETTS.]

BETTS. Right. Whichello will be here directly—— [*Taking out his watch.*]

FELIX. You're taking him on to meet Ben Chorley?

BETTS. Yes, the Socialists mean to be nasty. Chorley talks about running himself.

FELIX. He stands no earthly chance.

BETTS. No, but he can queer us. You may as well come on with us and see Chorley.

FELIX. Better not.

BETTS. Why not?

FELIX. I've been going about saying that the Liberal Party is the only bulwark against Socialism.

BETTS. What on earth made you say a damned silly thing like that?

FELIX. I had to say it. Socialism is a red rag to Borrodaile. You'd better not get in too deep with Chorley.

BETTS. My boy, we've got to win the seat, haven't we? You'll have to hedge over Socialism.

FELIX. We must keep in with Borrodaile ——

BETTS. We must muzzle Chorley.

FELIX. Very well. You tackle Chorley, and I'll butter Borrodaile.

BETTS. Right! Borrodaile, your pal — Chorley, mine.

Enter DAKIN, *showing in* MARY. *Exit* DAKIN.

MARY [*To* FELIX, *shaking hands*]. Good morning. [*To* BETTS.] Good morning, Mr. Betts. [*Shaking hands*.]

BETTS. Good morning.

MARY. My husband will be here in a moment. I must speak to you before he comes — no, don't go, Mr. Galpin — it's about the baronetcy ——

BETTS. Yes, but you know I'm only an understrapper. I'm the little boy who blows the organ. The Chief plays the tune. And the Chief is very touchy about the way these things are done. We've got to put on our moral frock coats and top hats, and avoid scandals.

MARY. But couldn't you give me some idea ——

BETTS. Of what?

MARY. Of how much it costs — for a baronetcy.

BETTS. Costs? The Chief's hair would turn white at the bare idea of any traffic in honors. There must be no bargain. But if Whichello wins the seat for us — and comes down handsomely for the Party funds ——

MARY. Yes ——

BETTS. The Chief is too good a chap to let his patriotism go unrewarded.

MARY. But you must remember that we already have a baronetcy in the Whichello family.

BETTS. Just now I don't fancy that would appeal so much to the Chief as hard cash. And if I could mention a tidy good round figure —— [*Watching her closely.*]

MARY. Oh, that will be all right. Quite all right. But Dick has got one of his stingy fits on. And he's in a very bad temper this morning. He's going to question you about the exact amount. You will give him some quite low estimate, so as not to upset him prematurely?

BETTS. But suppose he nails me to it afterwards?

MARY. Oh, he won't, will he, Mr. Galpin?

FELIX. I don't think Whichello is going to have much say in the matter.

MARY. Not when it comes to the crisis. You will mention quite a low figure —— [BETTS *demurs, and half shakes his head.*] Dear Mr. Betts, you must allow me to know him — Dick's the best husband in the world, but in money matters he always needs a — a — jumping board, before he takes the plunge.

BETTS. You're sure he'll jump when the time comes?

MARY. Oh, yes; won't he, Mr. Galpin?

FELIX. Like an antelope. I've seen him do it.

BETTS. Well, I'll put the matter before the Chief when I get back. I'm afraid a baronetcy may be doubtful. But the Chief might mention Whichello for a knighthood ——

MARY [*Offended*]. Knighthood? They give knighthoods to persons like the Bodsworths, and railway directors, and actors, and all sorts of people. We couldn't think of a knighthood.

BETTS. Well, we've got to win the seat first. Then we can talk about the trimmings.

MARY. And you will give Dick quite a low temporary estimate as a jumping board? [BETTS *looks doubtful.*] He will jump when the time comes.

BETTS. All right. Rely on me.

Enter DAKIN, *showing in* DICK *with paper in his pocket. Enter* DICK. *Exit* DAKIN.

DICK [*To* BETTS]. Good morning.

BETTS [*Shaking hands*]. Good morning.

DICK. How are you, Galpin?

FELIX. First rate.

DICK [*In a state of great irritation, pulling out paper*]. I say, I didn't go and make such a doddering ass of myself last night, did I? [*They are silent.*] Did I, Galpin?

FELIX. You weren't quite in your best fighting form.

DICK. No. Your speech went clean out of my head. But I got on very well, didn't I? [*They are silent.*] Anyway, I pulled up towards the end? Didn't I? Well, at any rate, I didn't make such a blathering idiot of myself as all this — [*pointing to paper*] — did I?

MARY [*Trying to take the paper away from him*]. You got on very well, indeed. I felt quite proud of you ——

DICK [*Keeping the paper*]. I don't want your

opinion. You've done nothing but egg me on from the first. What I want to know is this — did I make a silly jackass fool of myself last night, or did I not? I know jolly well I didn't. [*Throwing away the paper contemptuously.*] And I tell you this — I'm fed up with the whole business and the whole gang. Now, Mr. Betts, before you go any further I want to know what this is going to cost?

BETTS. Hadn't we better postpone that?

DICK. No. I'm not going to land myself in deuce knows what expense just for the pleasure of seeing B-a-r-t. stuck after my name. [*To* BETTS.] So if you please, you and I will have two minutes in private. Galpin, can we step in there?

FELIX. Certainly.

DICK [*Turning to* MARY]. And you kindly keep out of this. If I am going to be fleeced, I'll know how much. Now Mr. Betts ——

[BETTS *and* MARY *exchange a cheerful look of understanding as* DICK *goes up to curtains. Exeunt* BETTS *and* DICK *through curtains.*]

MARY [*Watching them off*]. That's all right. I shall have all the summer to get Dick to take the plunge. Is there anything more from the Herald's College?

FELIX. No. They're quite positive that your husband's family has no connection with the Kella-on Whichellos.

MARY. They haven't gone far enough back.

FELIX. They've gone back to the Civil War.

MARY. They must go back to the Conquest. think I'll go up to London and see them my-elf ——

FELIX. Yes, I would.

MARY. Who's the right man to get hold of?

FELIX. There's the Earl Marshal, three Kings at Arms, six Heralds, and four Pursuivants ——

MARY. What do the Pursuivants do?

FELIX. Oh, I suppose they hang about, and pur-ue anybody who sports a wrong coat-of-arms.

MARY. I'll get to know them. I might ask the Garter King at Arms and the Heralds to dinner ——

FELIX [*Has a shock of surprise, shrugs his shoulders ubiously*]. Yes. Well, the Garter King at Arms is our pal. But before you tackle him, what are you oing to do about the Bodsworth lawsuit?

MARY. Do? Nothing. Mr. Tadman hasn't served he writ yet?

FELIX. Not on me. You've heard nothing?

MARY. No. I don't believe they'll go on with it.

Ella shall call on Mrs. Bratwick and find out what's going on at the Bodsworths'.

FELIX. You're sure you can trust Mrs. Bratwick?

MARY. Oh, yes. I'm her bosom friend.

FELIX. I thought Lady Bodsworth was Mrs. Bratwick's bosom friend?

MARY. Yes, so she is. I'm her bosom friend, too. Ella is Mrs. Bratwick's extra special bosom friend. She tells Ella everything. "The impropriety" is raging like the heathen about the paragraphs in the *Mercury*. Have you seen it this morning?

FELIX. Not that column. [*Picks up the Liberal paper.*] "Warkinstall Society and Fashionable Gossip."

MARY. What a dear young fellow that is on the *Mercury* — so sympathetic.

FELIX [*Reading*]. "We understand that bright golden hair in large puffs will shortly become fashionable again, and will be extensively worn at the forthcoming assizes ——"

MARY [*Continuing*]. "We trust, however, that this attractive coiffure will not be carried to the point of impropriety" — Shush!

[*The curtains are pushed aside, and* DICK's
voice is heard.]

DICK [*Within the curtains*]. Very well, then;
that's clearly understood between us.

MARY. Don't show it to Dick. He's got enough
to bear this morning, poor dear!

DICK *and* BETTS *enter through curtains.*

BETTS [*To* DICK]. Of course you've got to win
the seat first. Then I'll talk to the Chief, and tell
him you are anxious to replenish the Party war-
chest ——

DICK. I'm not so anxious as all that. I've told
you my figure, and — [*nodding very emphatically at*
MARY]—I'm not going to be rushed for a penny more.

MARY [*Serenely*]. I'm so glad it's all arranged.
You shall tell me all about it when we get home.

DICK. I don't know that I shall. For once in a
way I'm going to manage my own affairs.

BETTS [*Taking out watch*]. We must be getting on
to Chorley.

DICK [*Plaintively*]. I haven't got to kow-tow to
Ben Chorley, have I?

BETTS. We shall have to skip gently round the
minimum wage.

[115]

DICK. Well, you skip gently round the minimum wage, and I'll skip gently round to the Golf Club. I've promised to meet Monkhouse at the station at eleven, and have a round on the Dunningtree course before lunch. I shall give Mr. Ben Chorley just ten minutes, no more.

Enter DAKIN.

DAKIN [*To* DICK]. Mr. Borrodaile is on the telephone, sir. He rang up at your house, and they told him you were here.

DICK [*Disgusted*]. What the nuisance is Boanerges rampaging about now?

DAKIN. He says he must see you this morning, sir.

DICK. Tell him to —— [*Bursts out.*] I'm not going to voice any more burning questions. I've been voicing burning questions for the last fortnight.

FELIX [*Looking up from the paper which he has been studying*]. I expect it's about last night's meeting. He rang me up an hour ago.

DICK. What did he say?

FELIX. He said you'd have to buckle on your armor, and gird up your loins.

DICK. Gird up my loins? Tell him to gird up his own loins — with that fat stomach of his.

FELIX. You'd better see him. He's got a very sore head.

DICK. Oh, well, you poultice it.

MARY. We'll ask him and Mrs. Borrodaile to dinner.

DICK. No, we will not ask them to dinner. Tea's their meal in my house. And I shan't be at home.

DAKIN [*Listening off*]. I fancy Mr. Borrodaile's ringing up again.

FELIX. He won't be happy till he has heckled you.

DICK [*Taking out watch*]. I shall give Boanerges Bloxam Borrodaile, D.D., five minutes; and I shall take it out of Ben Chorley's ten. Five minutes Chorley, five minutes Borrodaile. And then I'm off to golf. Now, Mr. Betts. [*Comes up against the Tory paper, snatches it up angrily.*] And there's this blackguard leading article — I know jolly well I never made such an ass of myself — I ——

[*Goes off muttering. Exit* DICK.

BETTS. If he keeps on jibbing at everything like this, we're dead certain to lose the seat.

[*Exit after* DICK.

[117]

FELIX [*Has been looking gravely at the Mercury*]. I say, don't you think you'd better stop this?

MARY. Stop my fashionable gossip? [*Takes out a little slip of paper from her bag.*] Listen to what I've got for to-morrow. [*Reads.*] "Ladies of a certain age who have too freely indulged in cosmetics should not discontinue the practice too suddenly. A magenta complexion, even if it is unseemly, may be less painful than a pasty 'au naturel.'"

FELIX. Yes, that's very good fun — if it only frightens Lady Bodsworth from going into Court. But suppose it doesn't? And suppose we get the wrong judge, and suppose it comes out that you've inspired these paragraphs?

MARY. What then?

FELIX. Well, then it won't be very good fun at all.

Enter DAKIN.

DAKIN. Mr. Tadman's clerk is here, sir, and he wishes to see Mrs. Whichello.

MARY. See me? What for?

DAKIN. He didn't mention his business, ma'am. They sent him on from your house. If you're busy he says he'll wait.

FELIX. Send him up, Dakin. [*Exit* DAKIN.

MARY. Why does Mr. Tadman send his clerk to me?

FELIX. Looks like a writ.

MARY. Then they are going on! And Mrs. Bratwick told Ella that Lady Bodsworth wanted to throw up the sponge and go abroad.

DAKIN *shows in* TADMAN's *clerk. Exit* DAKIN.

CLERK [*Bows to* MARY, *draws two sheets of paper from his pocket, goes to her, hands her one*]. Mrs. Whichello, I have to hand you this document which is a writ for slander brought on behalf of Lady Bodsworth. [MARY *looks at* FELIX *and reluctantly takes it.*] Here is the original if you wish to see it? [*Holding it out.*]

FELIX. That's all right, Pollard.

CLERK. Good morning, ma'am.

[*Bows to* FELIX. *Exit.*

MARY [*Reading, slurring the earlier words*]. "High Court of Justice . . . Grace of God, United Kingdom of Great Britain and Ireland, British Dominions beyond the Seas . . . Defender of the Faith . . . to Mary Sebright Whichello of the Cedars, St. John's Hill, Warkinstall . . .

[119]

County of . . . *We command you*, that within eight days after the service of this writ on you, you do cause an appearance to be entered for you ——"
[*Looking at* FELIX.]

FELIX. That isn't the sort of command you want.

MARY. "In an action at the suit of Frances Louisa, wife of Sir Thomas Bodsworth, Knight ——" We shall have to go on now ——

FELIX. If you do, that knocks your baronetcy on the head.

MARY. You think it does?

FELIX. If you want to get a baronetcy you mustn't be the defendant in a risky slander suit. That's pretty plain, isn't it?

MARY. But how can I help it?

FELIX. There's only one way. We shall have to back out and apologize.

MARY. Apologize? Never!

FELIX. Then bang goes the baronetcy.

MARY [*Takes a desperate turn, looks again at the writ*]. "And take notice that in default of your so doing, the Plaintiff may proceed therein, and judgment may be given in your absence. Witness, Richard Burdon, Viscount Haldane of Cloan, Lord High

Chancellor of Great Britain —— " There must be some way out of it.

FELIX. I don't see any.

MARY. Give up the baronetcy? Go in after that woman all my life? It's impossible.

FELIX. You can have the baronetcy, or you can have the lawsuit; but you can't have both. We must chuck the lawsuit. If we lose it, where are we? We shall all be discredited — Whichello for the seat, you for the title, and I get a bad kick, both as lawyer and election agent. We must draw out.

MARY. What had I better do?

FELIX. I'll run up against Tadman, and find out if they'll agree to a mild apology.

MARY. I won't apologize. [FELIX *shrugs his shoulders.*] You have got me into a horrible mess!

FELIX. I've got you into a horrible mess?

MARY. Well, haven't you? You've been advising me all through ——

FELIX. I've been trying to advise you ——

MARY. Yes, and see where you've landed me.

Enter DAKIN.

DAKIN. Mr. Tadman is below, sir. He'd like to speak to you and Mrs. Whichello.

[121]

FELIX [*After a glance at* MARY]. Show him up. [*Exit* DAKIN.] You'd better not say anything. Let me arrange it if I can.

MARY. I'm not going to apologize — at least, not till the last moment.

FELIX. We'll hear what he has to say. Shush!

Enter DAKIN, *showing in* TADMAN. *Exit* DAKIN.

FELIX. Good morning, Tadman.

TADMAN [*Very cordial*]. Good morning. [*Goes to* MARY.] Good morning, dear Mrs. Whichello.

MARY. Good morning.

TADMAN. I must apologize for intruding, Galpin. I've been walking up and down outside your gate for ten minutes ——

FELIX. Taking exercise?

TADMAN. No. I was coming down from Sir Thomas when my clerk Pollard came out after doing his duty. [*Tapping the writ in* MARY's *hand*.] He mentioned you were here. And I said to myself, "Now, shall I do a rather unprofessional thing, and make one last attempt to keep this out of Court?" And I said, "I will, just for the sake of my old friendship with Whichello."

FELIX. That was kind of you. Sit down, won't you?

TADMAN. No, thanks. Can't stay. Got to be back at my office.

FELIX. Sir Thomas doesn't know you're here?

TADMAN. Of course I shall tell him. And I'm sure he'll see I'm not acting against his interest in taking this upon myself. [*A pause.*] You've looked through that? [*Signifying writ.*]

MARY. Not all through. I don't understand lawyers' language.

FELIX. It was a long time coming, Tadman. We began to think you'd forgotten all about it.

TADMAN. I held it back, thinking that perhaps Mrs. Whichello might be inclined to — a ——

MARY. I'm not going to apologize.

TADMAN. If you've quite made up your mind — I'm sorry. I hoped perhaps —— [*Going toward door.* FELIX *makes an appeal to* MARY *behind his back.* MARY *responds with a gesture of dissent.*] Good morning. [*Opens door, going.*

FELIX. Tadman, if I were to advise Mrs. Whichello ——

MARY. Oh, I couldn't! Not apologize!

TADMAN [*Coming toward her*]. If I might suggest — we're all old friends — we don't want to wash our dirty linen in public ——

MARY. Oh, it isn't my dirty linen. And I'm not washing it.

TADMAN. No, but you'll have to pay the laundry bill. And you and Whichello will get thoroughly splashed. He wants to go into Parliament, doesn't he?

MARY. Not very much. But I think I shall get him there.

TADMAN [*Pointing to writ*]. Won't that be rather in your way?

MARY. Oh, no! I've been canvassing. The voters love to talk about yellow hair and magenta cheeks. They like it better than politics.

> [FELIX, *behind* TADMAN's *back, shakes his head severely at* MARY *and shows despair.*]

TADMAN. Well, I've done my best. It's a pity. [*Going toward door.* FELIX *makes another appeal to* MARY.] Good morning.

FELIX. What do you propose?

TADMAN. Nothing. But whatever you propose I'll ask Sir Thomas to consider favorably.

FELIX. Hadn't you better get Sir Thomas's authority?

TADMAN [*Shakes his head*]. In his present temper he won't listen to anything but a definite apology.

If I could take him a form we had arranged upon he might give way — I can't tell — I'm willing to try it.

> [FELIX *looks at* MARY. TADMAN *looks from one to the other.*]

MARY [*After a longish pause*]. I'll think it over.

TADMAN [*Shakes his head*]. I'm on my way to engage counsel. When that is done an apology will be too late.

MARY [*Very reluctantly, after a pause*]. I don't mind saying I'm sorry.

TADMAN. I daren't approach Sir Thomas with anything but a formal apology, with an expression of regret, and an assurance not to repeat.

FELIX. For publication?

TADMAN. Except in case of necessity I should advise Sir Thomas not to publish.

MARY. No, but the "impropriety" — [FELIX *shakes his head at* MARY] — would show it all over the town.

FELIX. What form do you suggest?

TADMAN. I must just consider that. Let me run down to the Club, and draw up the easiest terms I can advise Sir Thomas to accept. Then if you and Mrs. Whichello approve I can go straight to Sir

Thomas; we can sign it to-day and the matter's ended.

MARY [*After a pause, very reluctantly*]. Very well.

TADMAN. I've done you and Whichello a good turn. I'll be back soon.

MARY [*As* TADMAN *is going off and is closing door, calls after him*]. It must be very mild, not like your other apology — just a tiny wee one.

[*Exit* TADMAN.

MARY. There! You see what you've let me in for.

FELIX. I've let you in?

MARY. You should have bluffed Mr. Tadman.

FELIX. Yes, and bluffed you out of all chance of the baronetcy. Now we've got to put some stiffening into Whichello. He's going the right way to lose this election. We must coax him to swallow the minimum wage from Chorley. And above all we've got to keep him good pals with Borrodaile.

DICK *enters in a towering rage.* *They look at him.*

MARY. Dick! What's the matter?

DICK. I've had twenty mortal minutes with Bloxam Borrodaile.

MARY [*Alarmed*]. You haven't quarreled with him?

[126]

DICK. Not outwardly and visibly. But inwardly I have consigned him to bottomless perdition. And if he crosses my path within the next three months —— [*Moves his fist slowly up and down, threatening the absent* BORRODAILE. MARY *and* FELIX *look at each other in despair.* FELIX *shrugs his shoulders and goes away.*]

MARY. What did he do?

DICK. He boanerged all over his drawing-room, like a bull of Basham; lathered me for my speech last night, and wants me to take the chair next week for some black chap who's going to voice the wrongs of India.

MARY. You said you would?

DICK. No, I did not. I sloped off to the station and left him boanerging on his doorstep. When I got to the station the Dunningtree train had gone. So he has done me out of my round with Monkhouse. [*Turns solemnly to* MARY.] Now, don't you ask Bloxam Borrodaile to my house. His tea's off.

MARY. But we must keep in with Borrodaile—— [*Appeals to* FELIX, *who shrugs his shoulders and grins.*]

DICK. You keep in with him if you like, but

speaking for myself, two penn'orth more of Borrodaile, and I throw up the whole job.

MARY [*In despair*]. Throw up? You can't throw up your Liberal principles now! [*Again appeals to* FELIX, *who shrugs his shoulders and grins.*]

DICK. Can't I? Two penn'orth more of Borrodaile — one penn'orth — a hea'porth ——

Enter DAKIN.

DAKIN [*To* DICK]. Mr. Borrodaile wants to speak to you again on the 'phone, sir.

[FELIX *bursts into laughter.* DICK *rises, furious; thinks better of it, and calmly sits down.*]

DICK. Tell him I'll make an appointment with him in the sweet by and by.

MARY. No — no — you must go and see what he wants, mustn't he? [*Appeals to* FELIX, *who merely shrugs his shoulders and grins.*]

DAKIN. He says it's most important, sir; something he forgot to question you about ——

DICK. Tell him to heckle the telephone. I've had enough of it.

MARY [*To* DAKIN]. Tell him Mr. Whichello will be down to speak to him in a moment.

[*Exit* DAKIN

MARY [*Trying to get* DICK *out of his chair*]. Now, Dick, we can't win the election without Borrodaile.

DICK. Then we'll lose it.

MARY. But if we lose the election we shan't get the baronetcy. We can't lose it! [*Tries again to get* DICK *out of the chair, appeals with a gesture to* FELIX.] Mr. Galpin, won't you —— Please!

FELIX. I'll go and see what Borrodaile wants.

MARY. Tell him Dick agrees with every word he says. [FELIX *goes off. She calls after him.*] And tell him I'll take the chair for his black man. Now, Dick, this is disgraceful! You knew what it meant when you took up Liberal principles ——

DICK. By Jove, I didn't! or I'd never have gone in for it.

MARY. But you have gone in for it. You said you'd never draw back. You said you wouldn't let Bodsworth walk over you.

DICK. Well, he isn't going to walk over me.

MARY. But he is walking over you. You must go on now! You must fight it to the end!

DICK. Very well then, if you want me to see this through, you keep Borrodaile out of my way, because if he dares to boanerge over me, I shall gird up my loins and I shall —— Good heavens!

MARY. What is the matter?

DICK. Good Lord!

MARY. What is it?

DICK. I've lost my golf clubs. [MARY *looks at him in despair*.] Now that's all through jawing with Borrodaile about his black man! Now where did I — I must have left them at the station.

Reënter FELIX

MARY. What does Mr. Borrodaile want?

FELIX. It seems two members of his congregation saw Whichello playing golf on Sunday. He says no man is fit to represent Warkinstall on Liberal principles who plays golf on Sundays. And unless — [*to* DICK] — you give a distinct pledge to abstain from Sunday golf, he must request you to resign your candidature.

DICK. That's all right. I resign my candidature.

MARY. No! [*Glancing nervously at* DICK.] Tell him Mr. Whichello will abstain ——

DICK [*Jumps up*]. Eh?

MARY. Tell him it will be all right. [*Glancing nervously at* DICK.] Ask him to bring Mrs. Borrodaile to have din — [DICK *looks furious*] — tea with me ——

DICK. Not in my house.

MARY. Say it will be all right, and ask him and Mrs. Borrodaile to dinner with you to-night.

FELIX. Dinner with me?

MARY. Yes — I'll come, too. Oh, do go and pacify him! do! [*Getting him off at door, looks at* DICK, *who is placidly lighting a cigarette; can't quite make up her mind how to tackle him.*] Dick, you deserve to be shaken! [*Rushes furiously at him and shakes him.*] You can't really mean to draw back now?

DICK. Yes, I do. I wash my hands of the whole crew.

MARY. No. Not till you've won the seat. *Wheedling.*] You will keep in with Borrodaile till after the election? Yes — there's a dear, good boy! And I'll be such a darling to you for a long while. I've always said you were the best husband in the world ——

DICK [*Has picked up the cigarette she has knocked out of his hand*]. Well, so I am.

MARY. Yes, if you'll only just let me, eh? — *stroking his chin and kissing him*] — eh? — phone to old Boanerges that you'll give up the golf — eh? old sonnie, eh?

[131]

DICK. Give up my golf? After sticking in the House all the week, listening to their jaw half the night, and voting just how I'm told for a lot of hangnation things I don't know and don't care a cuss about! No. We're in this world for a very short time. Do let us be happy, do let us be comfortable while we are here.

MARY. You'll be more chaffed than ever! You will have a bad time —— [*Goes to him again, throws her arms round his neck.*] Dick, old man, give it to me for a birthday present next month, eh?

DICK. Give you what?

MARY. Let me see Borrodaile and Ben Chorley and promise them everything they want. I'll do it all — and get you safely into the House, and then as soon as the Government have rewarded you, you can retire from politics, and go round the world. And when you come back, you can change your views and be a nice old Tory again, and join your club — eh?

DICK [*Calm, good-humored, very firm*]. No. No. No. No. No.

MARY. You mean that? You aren't going to fight the seat after all?

DICK [*Same tone*]. No. No. No. No. No. No.

[MARY *bursts suddenly into tears.*]

[132]

MARY [*Sobbing*]. And after all I've done for you. And the Duchess of Gloucester is coming to open the maternity wing of the Sanatorium. And Lady Bodsworth is going to present her with a bouquet. [*Peeping at him through her tears.*] I shall go and stay with Aunt Henrietta! You won't like that! Remember how you begged me to come home last time. I'll stay away for a month! I will! [*Peeping at him. He remains unmoved, placidly smoking. She rushes at him.*] Dick, you're a brute!

DICK. Now, look here, old girl. I'm not going into Parliament. That's settled. But next month, when your birthday comes, we'll go to the South ——

MARY. No, we won't.

DICK. Well, where shall we go? Don't you remember the jolly times we had at ——

MARY. No!

DICK. Well, we have had some jolly times together. [MARY *dissents*.] Oh yes, we have. [*Trying to fondle her.*] And I'll give you that new Rolls Royce, and I'll take you for the jolliest trip — now where shall we go?

MARY. I'm going to Aunt Henrietta the first thing to-morrow morning.

FELIX *enters.*

MARY. What did you tell Mr. Borrodaile?

FELIX. They'd cut us off, and his line's engaged. What's the matter?

MARY. He has thrown it up! The maundering renegade! The turncoat! The incoherent and incapable wobbler! The blustering and blundering ratter! Look at him!

[DICK *sits quietly smoking.*]

FELIX. You aren't to stand for Warkinstall?

DICK [*Same tone*]. No. No. No. No. No. No.

FELIX. What's to be done?

MARY. They ought to make him a baronet for the cemetery.

FELIX. Not much chance of that.

MARY. Then he must give the town something else — a new Town Hall!

FELIX. We don't want a new Town Hall.

MARY. Well, what does the town want? A people's park with zoölogical gardens and tortoises and kangaroos and a monkey house ——

DICK. With land all round at two thousand pounds an acre. No, thank you!

MARY. Well — a picture gallery — a museum — an aquarium? The town must want something.

Enter BETTS.

BETTS. It's all right. I've nobbled Chorley. [*To* DICK.] But you'll have to swallow the minimum wage and the Osborne judgment.

DICK. I'm not going to swallow anything!

MARY [*Calling* BETTS *to her*]. Mr. Betts, my husband thinks that perhaps the Liberal cause might not be quite safe in his hands, so he has decided to become a philanthropist to the town.

BETTS [*Looks all round, puzzled*]. Oh! Has he?

MARY [*Drawing* BETTS *aside*]. Rather than the Liberal cause should suffer through him, he'll sacrifice himself —— [*Goes on talking to* BETTS.]

DICK. I say, Galpin, I've lost my golf clubs ——

FELIX. Have you?

DICK. I can't remember where I left them. I know I had them in the cab when I left Borrodaile's. I believe I took them into the booking office. Would you let your man ring them up at the station, and ask them to look round?

FELIX. Certainly.

DICK. I haven't had a round for a fortnight, ever

since this ghastly speeching and voicing has been going on.

BETTS [*To* MARY]. Oh, no, I couldn't suggest it. We can't go chucking about titles for museums and picture galleries. We're out to win the seat from the Tories. Seats are what we want just now!

MARY. Then what's to be done? [*Sees* FELIX, *is struck with an idea.*] Mr. Galpin, you must stand for Warkinstall!

FELIX. Stand for Warkingstall!

BETTS [*Enthusiastically*]. Good business! Good business!

MARY. What do you say?

FELIX. Oh, I'm on the job — emphatically on the job. But I've got no money.

MARY. Dick and I will see to that.

DICK. What?

MARY. Of course, you will, Dick. You can't leave the Liberal Party in the lurch now. You're bound to see them through this election. [*Turns to* BETTS.] If Mr. Whichello lends his influence to Mr. Galpin, and pays the election expenses, I suppose the Chief would recognize his self-sacrifice?

BETTS. I feel sure he would. I should explain Whichello's self-denying action, and if he'll — [*look-*

[136]

ing at DICK] — send a tidy cheque to the war-chest, I'll put it in the right light to the Chief.

MARY.   Then that's settled.

DICK.   I don't know so much about that.

MARY.   Hold your tongue, Dick.   [*In a very low pleading voice to* BETTS.]   I suppose if my husband sent in quite a large cheque — something very handsome indeed — the Government would consider him for — a ——

BETTS.   For what?

MARY [*In a very timid, nervous whisper*].   For a — peerage?

BETTS.   Peerage?   [*By a gesture expresses horror too great to be conveyed in words.*]

MARY.   I said of course they wouldn't.   Of course not.   We shall be quite satisfied with a baronetcy.

DICK.   Mr. Betts, you know my figure.   [*To* MARY.]   Not a penny more.   Now can I get on to the station about my golf clubs?

MARY [*In a low tone to* BETTS].   It's all right.   He will jump.   [*To* FELIX.]   Will Mr. Borrodaile accept you as candidate?

FELIX.   Oh, yes.   After my speech last night he wrung my hand and said: "Ah, Mr. Galpin, you're the sort of man we want to blow the Liberal trumpet in Warkinstall and Westminster!"

BETTS. I say, old man, you'll have to play a tune or two on the Socialist trumpet ——

FELIX. Shall I?

BETTS. I've promised Chorley ——

FELIX. That's awkward. I've been telling everybody that the Liberal Party is the only bulwark against Socialism.

MARY. Well, isn't it?

FELIX. I dunno. That's what I've been saying.

MARY. Never mind what you've been saying. You've got to win the seat.

FELIX [*After a perplexed gesture*]. Well, after all it's only looking at things from a Socialist point of view ——

DICK [*Who has been quietly smoking and ruminating, has just taken up the writ and glanced at it*]. Hillo, Galpin, what's this?

FELIX. What?

DICK. You've told me all through I shouldn't have a lawsuit with Bodsworth.

FELIX. I hope I shall be able to arrange ——

DICK. You'd better, because if this comes into

Court I button up my pockets for the election expenses.

[FELIX *looks appealingly at* MARY.]

DAKIN *shows in* ELLA, *and exits.*

ELLA [*Dancing in*]. She's funked it! She's funked it! She's funked it!

MARY. Who has? Funked what?

ELLA. The "impropriety." She daren't go into Court! She simply daren't!

MARY. How do you know?

ELLA. Mrs. Bratwick has just called with the joyful news, so I came on with it at once.

MARY. Yes — tell me ——

ELLA. It seems they had a grand council of war last night ——

MARY. Who?

ELLA. Sir Thomas, the "impropriety," and Mr. Tadman. Sir Thomas wanted to go on, but she daren't face it, so they decided to withdraw from the lawsuit.

MARY. But they've sent me a writ.

ELLA. Yes. The "impropriety" wants an apology. So Tadman suggested he should serve the writ, and then call upon you, as an old friend, and get an apology out of you if he could.

[139]

MARY. The old fox! We might have known he was bluffing.

ELLA. So he's coming to see you this morning to try it on.

MARY. Is he? Is he?

ELLA. Don't you let him get round you.

MARY. Oh, I won't.

ELLA. The "impropriety" has decided to have an attack of rheumatism and be ordered to Aix. That's to be their reason for not going on with the lawsuit.

Enter DAKIN, *showing in* TADMAN. *Exit* DAKIN.

TADMAN. Morning, Whichello.

DICK. Good morning.

TADMAN. Good morning, Miss Southwood.

ELLA. Good morning.

TADMAN [*Drawing out a sheet of paper*]. I'm delighted we're going to settle this painful little affair.

MARY. So are we.

TADMAN [*Giving* FELIX *the paper*]. I've made it quite easy for Mrs. Whichello. I think that will meet the case.

FELIX [*Glancing at paper*]. I don't think so, Tadman, I don't think so.

[140]

TADMAN [*Surprised*]. Eh?

MARY. How is Lady Bodsworth this morning?

TADMAN. Very well, I believe.

MARY. No symptoms of her old enemy, rheumatism?

TADMAN. No. Won't you look at the apology?

MARY. It won't be necessary, will it, Mr. Galpin?

FELIX. Not at all. You may tell Sir Thomas we accept service of the writ.

TADMAN [*Nonplussed*]. Oh! That is your final decision?

FELIX. Absolutely.

TADMAN. I may warn you ——

FELIX. No, don't, Tadman. [*Putting his hand on* TADMAN's *shoulder*.] You go to Sir Thomas and Lady Bodsworth, as an old friend, and say we shall fight this out in Court.

MARY. Wigs on the green!

TADMAN. Oh! [*Looks round.*] I'll tell Sir Thomas. Good morning. [*Exit* TADMAN.

MARY [*To* GALPIN]. Now, you must get out your election address.

FELIX. Right.

MARY. Can I help you?

FELIX. Rather. We must pitch it strong.

Enter DAKIN *with a set of golf sticks.*

DAKIN [*To* DICK]. The cabman who took you to the station found these in the cab, sir.

DICK [*Taking his golf clubs lovingly*]. Give him half-a-crown. [*Exit* DAKIN.

MARY. Dick, you must get out a farewell address to the electors, recommending Mr. Galpin.

DICK. Eh?

FELIX. Don't worry about that. I'll write it for you.

[MARY, ELLA, *and* FELIX *have had a hurried talk.* FELIX *sits down to write,* MARY *over him.*]

DICK [*Strapping his clubs on his shoulder*]. Now look here, Galpin. I'm not going to be landed in goodness knows what expenses over this confounded election of yours ——

MARY [*Waving him away*]. Run away, you dear thing! Run away, and play golf till after the election.

FELIX. Fellow citizens of Warkinstall ——

[DICK *is going off with his clubs on his shoulder.*]

Curtain.

[142]

EPILOGUE

Nearly two years and a half pass between Act III and the Epilogue

EPILOGUE

SCENE: *The same. The room has been brightened by the addition of feminine belongings, and gives evidence that there is a mistress in the house.*

TIME: *Just before dinner on a summer evening. The room is dimly lighted. The blind is up and the last rays of the setting sun come through the window.*

Discover FELIX *and* CHESHER *in evening dress, as if waiting for guests.* DAKIN *is making the room tidy, and turns up additional electric lights.*

FELIX. So Ella and I thought we'd give a little dinner, and get them to shake hands and bury the hatchet.

CHESHER. Then you're friendly with the Bodsworths?

FELIX. My dear uncle, I'm member for Warkinstall, and I intend to remain member for Warkinstall, so Ella and I are friendly with everybody.

DAKIN [*Going off*]. I beg pardon, sir — shall I throw it up a bit?

FELIX. Throw what up?

DAKIN [*In a rather loud tone*]. Sir Richard and Lady Whichello.

FELIX. No, Dakin, no. Keep that tone for knighthoods. The higher the title the less it needs throwing up.

DAKIN. Yes, sir. [*Exit.*

FELIX. Yes, Ella and I had been trying to bring them together for months.

CHESHER. Should have thought two years rowing would have satisfied any reasonable people.

FELIX. It was Lady Bodsworth who held off. Bodsworth is ready to make it up, because he and Tadman are working Tariff Reform, and they want Dick to join them in getting a stiff duty on leather goods out of the Tory leaders.

CHESHER. What are Whichello's politics just now?

FELIX. Rather northwest southeast. Well, six weeks ago, Lady Bodsworth fortunately had a motor accident about twenty miles out. Dick and Mary fortunately came by and picked her up and carried her to the nearest inn. Dick and Mary had just got a note from the Prime Minister to say they were to be included in the birthday honors. So Mary was very kind; stayed with Lady Bodsworth all night, and nursed her up rather more than she wanted to be nursed. Now Mary has got the baronetcy, she feels rather friendly toward Lady Bodsworth.

CHESHER. There's nobody we like quite so much as the enemy we have thoroughly downed.

FELIX. Well, that paved the way for a reconciliation. But Ella had no end of a job to persuade Lady Bodsworth to come to-night. However, she is coming; and we are going to have a jolly little family dinner party. That's why I invited you down. You'll be in at the death.

CHESHER. Doctor's chief function.

Enter DAKIN, *announcing* MR. *and* MRS. TADMAN.
Enter TADMAN *and* MRS. TADMAN. *Exit* DAKIN.

FELIX [*To* MRS. TADMAN]. How d'ye do? [*Shaking hands.*]

MRS. T. How d'ye do?

FELIX. My wife will be down directly. We were late in getting back from the Petbury garden party.

[CHESHER *and* TADMAN *have shaken hands*.
　　　MRS. TADMAN *shakes hands with* CHESHER.]

FELIX. Tadman, how are you?

TADMAN [*Rosier, more shaky*]. Never felt so well in my life.

FELIX. There's a bottle of your own port for you.

TADMAN. Then I shall feel better still.

FELIX. And you'll find a cocktail on that table. [*Pointing to window.*]

TADMAN. Thanks. [*Helping himself to cocktail.*]

MRS. T. I'm so sorry the Bodsworths aren't coming.

FELIX [*Taken aback*]. Not coming?

MRS. T. You haven't heard?

FELIX. No, we're expecting them.

MRS. T. Perhaps I oughtn't to have spoken.

FELIX. Yes — please tell me.

MRS. T. I was calling on Lady Bodsworth this afternoon. She was very much upset.

FELIX. What about?

MRS. T. Sir Thomas and she were not invited to the garden party at Petbury Park this afternoon.

FELIX. I can't help that. There were only the county people there.

MRS. T. She feels it was a great slight, and she

[148]

couldn't possibly dine with you under the circumstances.

FELIX. But good heavens! I can't tell Lady Petbury whom to invite ——

MRS. T. So I told her, but she wouldn't be persuaded. I left her writing a note to Mrs. Galpin, asking you to excuse them.

FELIX. Well, of all — it's really too bad ——

TADMAN [*Over his cocktail*]. Never mind, Galpin! If the dinner is up to your usual standard, we shall get on very well without the Bodsworths.

FELIX. But we're giving this dinner on purpose to bring them and the Whichellos together again.

CHESHER. Felix, my boy, you don't seem quite to hit it off with your dinner parties.

FELIX. And Lady Bodsworth fixed the day herself — they might have sent us word to say they weren't coming — it's too bad.

TADMAN [*Has been looking out of the window*]. Isn't that the Bodsworth motor just driven up? Yes ——

[MRS. TADMAN *and* CHESHER *move toward window.*]

MRS. T. Sir Thomas is getting out.

FELIX. Is he alone?

TADMAN. No — there's Lady Bodsworth — he's helping her out ——

MRS. T. So they're coming after all.

TADMAN. There's something the matter.

MRS. T. Lady Bodsworth is crying.

FELIX. I suppose we shall have a scene again.

MRS. T. She is getting back into the motor.

TADMAN. No, Sir Thomas won't let her. He's arguing with her.

MRS. T. Oh, yes, she is coming in. Let's hope it will all pass off pleasantly.

> [MRS. TADMAN, CHESHER, *and* FELIX *come away from the window.*]

FELIX. Uncle, I think Ella has arranged for you to take her in.

CHESHER. I scarcely feel equal to it.

TADMAN [*Has helped himself to another cocktail*]. Oh, give her a glass or two of Galpin's champagne to start with.

FELIX. And keep off the Whichello baronetcy. And the Petbury garden party.

MRS. T. Yes, and she's very touchy about — but, perhaps I oughtn't to mention it ——

FELIX. Oh, yes! Let's make her happy if we can. What's she touchy about?

MRS. T. Well, as you know, the last two years since your dinner party everybody has been making remarks about the way she does her hair, and it makes her very sensitive. She had got a new transformation for to-night, but Sir Thomas wouldn't let her wear it. He insists that for the future she shall wear her own hair.

FELIX. Good Lord! What will she look like now?

MRS. T. Well, I told her it suited her beautifully.

FELIX. Oh! let's all tell her it suits her beautifully.

MRS. T. No! She's so fidgety, we'd better pretend to take no notice.

FELIX. Oh, let us all pretend anything — if it will only keep her quiet.

Enter DAKIN, *announcing* SIR THOMAS BODSWORTH.
Enter SIR THOMAS. DAKIN *waits.* FELIX *advances to shake hands with* SIR THOMAS.

FELIX. How d'ye do, Sir Thomas? We hope Lady Bodsworth ——

SIR T. [*Shaking hands*]. Lady Bodsworth is overtaken with the heat. She is in the morning-room.

[151]

She asked me to come up and leave her to recover herself. Please don't take any notice.

FELIX. We are so sorry ——

SIR T. It's nothing. She'll be here in a minute. [*Goes to* TADMAN, MRS. TADMAN, *and* CHESHER, *and shakes hands with them.*]

FELIX. Dakin, will you send up to Mrs. Galpin and say our guests are arriving.

DAKIN. I beg pardon, sir, Mrs. Galpin was coming downstairs, when she heard Lady Bodsworth upsetting herself. She is now in the morning-room pacifying Lady Bodsworth.

FELIX. Oh, all right.

[*Much perplexed, looking anxiously at his watch. Exit* DAKIN.]

TADMAN [*Has been talking with* SIR THOMAS]. We'll ask Galpin. [*Comes up, cocktail in hand.*] Galpin, now we're all tiled in, and all friends, how much did Whichello stump up for his baronetcy?

FELIX [*Warningly*]. Shush-sh-sh-sh. Nobody can say that he didn't richly deserve it.

SIR T. Oh, certainly. We are all delighted at the honor, particularly Lady Bodsworth and myself. Nobody who knows the burden of a title, the amount of public duty it entails — and the subscriptions to

[152]

charities, would envy those whom it pleases his Majesty to select for the honor.

CHESHER. My old fellow-student, Sir Robert Latimore, got a baronetcy last year to please his wife. Bob declares that if he hadn't been obliged to work so hard for the title, he might have known something about medicine.

TADMAN. Now, between ourselves, Galpin, how much did Whichello ——

FELIX. [*Warningly*]. Shush-sh-sh! Shush-sh-sh!

TADMAN. We shall get him again, Galpin — we shall get him again!

FELIX. Who?

TADMAN. He's wobbling! He's wobbling! Bet you a new hat we shall have him safe in the Tory fold before he's a year older.

LADY BODSWORTH *enters, accompanied by* ELLA. LADY BODSWORTH *is wearing her own hair, which is gray-white and rather scanty. She is recovering from a fit of crying, and has a little smudged her complexion.* ELLA *is comforting and supporting her.*

ELLA. There! There! You're better now. [*Taking her to sofa,— and seating her.*]

[153]

LADY B. I do hope everybody will excuse me —— [*Weeping a little.*]

ELLA. Oh, yes. Sit there a minute. We'll leave you to come round.

> [*Exchanges a look of comic distress with* FELIX, *who goes to* LADY BODSWORTH *and shakes hands with her.* ELLA *goes to* SIR THOMAS *and the* TADMANS, *and shakes hands.* LADY BODSWORTH *remains on sofa weeping.*]

Ella. How are you, Sir Thomas. [*Shaking hands.*] Dear Mrs. Tadman. [*Shaking hands.*] Mr. Tadman, how are you? [*Shaking hands.*] Uncle, so glad you could run down. [*Shaking hands with* CHESHER.] You must please forgive me being late. We could not get away from the Petbury garden party ——

> [*A little choking sob from* LADY BODSWORTH, *who sits on sofa.* TADMAN, MRS. TADMAN, *and* CHESHER *admonish* ELLA *to silence by a look.* SIR THOMAS *is vexed at* LADY BODSWORTH'S *behavior, and frowns at her to be quiet.*]

ELLA [*Can't understand the meaning of the look the* TADMANS *and* CHESHER *have given her — goes on*]. It was such a jolly party ——

> [LADY BODSWORTH *has another rather louder*

choke. The TADMANS *again admonish* ELLA
to silence by a look. ELLA *doesn't under-*
stand. The TADMANS *and* CHESHER *draw*
her a little aside and explain in dumb show.
FELIX *has tried to comfort* LADY BODS-
WORTH.]

LADY B. [*Between her sobs, to* FELIX]. You're very
kind, but I really think I'd better go home.

SIR T. [*Sternly*]. Nonsense! Nonsense! We have
come expressly to congratulate Sir Richard and
Lady Whichello upon the honor which it has pleased
his Majesty to confer upon them. [*Goes to her and
argues.* FELIX *is seen to be comforting her.*]

ELLA [*To* TADMANS *and* CHESHER]. I see. I
won't mention the garden party. And there's another thing. Sir Thomas has made her wear her own
hair, and she's fretting because she thinks it isn't
becoming.

TADMAN. It's a good deal more becoming than—

MRS. T. Shush — don't look at her — she'll
guess we're talking about it.

TADMAN. Mum! Mum!

    [*He goes to table, puts down his second cock-
tail empty, hesitates whether he shall take a
third.* SIR THOMAS *has frightened* LADY

BODSWORTH *into submission.* FELIX *looks impatiently at his watch and comes to* ELLA.]

ELLA [*To* FELIX]. The dinner will be spoilt.

LADY B. [*Plaintively, from sofa*]. I suppose there were a great many people at the garden party?

FELIX. No. Just a few staunch Liberals like myself.

ELLA. Mary and Dick ought to be here ——

Enter DAKIN, *announcing* SIR RICHARD *and* LADY WHICHELLO. *Enter* MARY *and* DICK. *Exit* DAKIN.

MARY. My dear Ella, we're terribly late. Ah, my dear Sir Thomas! Now this is really good of you [*Shaking hands*].

SIR T. We are delighted to congratulate you and Sir Richard ——

MARY. I'm sure you are —— [*Stops at seeing* LADY BODSWORTH, *who, upon her entrance, has had a renewed little fit of tears*.]

SIR T. [*In reply to an inquiring look from* MARY]. It's nothing — a little overtaken by the heat — please take no notice.

MARY. You really must excuse us, Ella — the

Petburys would keep us till the last moment —— [LADY BODSWORTH *has a louder choking sob* — TADMAN, ELLA, CHESHER, *and* MRS. TADMAN *admonish* MARY *by a look to keep quiet.*] And as they were giving the party in our honor — [*Another look from the group, which* MARY *doesn't understand*] — we felt bound to stay till the last moment. [*Another look from the group. To* ELLA.] What's the matter?

[ELLA *whispers to* MARY.]

SIR T. [*Sternly to* LADY BODSWORTH]. Now, Fanny, my dear, rouse yourself — and offer our sincere congratulations to Sir Richard and Lady Whichello upon the honor which it has pleased his Majesty ——

[LADY BODSWORTH *rises, still tearful, tries to speak, bursts into tears.*]

MARY. Oh, never mind about the congratulations. Dick and I are tired of them. [*To* LADY BODSWORTH.] Now this is very dear of you and Sir Thomas. We're so glad to meet you again as old friends —— [*Shaking hands.*]

LADY B. [*Still tearful, nerving herself to speak.*] I'm sure we're delighted — delighted —— [*Has a renewed little fit of tears.*]

MARY. Of course you are. And we shall see a great deal of you, I hope. Lady Petbury sent you such a sweet message.

LADY B. Did she?

MARY. Yes, she said: "How is our dear Lady Bodsworth? I must call and see her the first time I'm in Warkinstall."

LADY B. I think she might have invited —— [*Sinking on the sofa in renewed sobs.*] I do feel I've been slighted.

MARY. No, no, no ——

> [LADY BODSWORTH *continues sobbing.* MARY *turns round with a gesture of helplessness to the company.*]

LADY B. I'm sorry to upset your party ——

ELLA. Oh, don't mention it. [*To* FELIX.] The dinner's spoiling.

SIR T. [*Sternly*]. Fanny, this is unworthy the dignity of our position. Even if we are not invited to Petbury, we have still our rank in Warkinstall to maintain. Remember that, and don't let me have to blush for you.

> [MARY *goes to* LADY BODSWORTH, *and is seen to be fussing over her and comforting her.*]

[158]

TADMAN. Oh, before I forget, Whichello, just put that in your pocket and look at it when you get home. [*Giving paper.*]

DICK. What is it?

TADMAN. My revised scheme of Tariff Reform. I've eased a bit on bacon, and tightened on rubber and mackintosh.

DICK. So long as the leather trade gets a look-in ——

TADMAN. Oh, it does. That's a water-tight scheme. I've sent it to the Party leaders.

DICK. Good!

TADMAN. And we hope you'll attend the meeting and say a few words ——

DICK. No, thank you. I've chucked politics. Let everybody have everything he hollers for. Then we shall all be happy.

[MARY *has taken* LADY BODSWORTH *apart, and is comforting her.*]

LADY B. You're quite sure it suits me?

MARY. Perfectly, perfectly. I've never seen you look so charming. Don't change it in the least.

[ELLA *has whispered to* SIR THOMAS *and* TAD-MAN *about their partners.*]

[159]

Enter DAKIN.

DAKIN. Dinner is served, ma'am. [*Exit* DAKIN.

MARY [*To* LADY BODSWORTH]. There! You feel better now.

LADY B. [*A little tearful still*]. Yes, but —— [*Gulps.* ELLA *comes up to* LADY BODSWORTH *and whispers to her.*]

LADY B. [*Discontentedly*]. Oh, Mr. Tadman takes me in ——

FELIX [*To* ELLA]. I thought my uncle ——

CHESHER. Oh, I give way and come in on my own. Mr. Tadman ——

   [TADMAN, *after much hesitation, is just putting
    his third cocktail to his lips, hurriedly puts
    glass on table, and goes to* LADY BODSWORTH,
    offers his arm.]

TADMAN. Delighted.

   [LADY BODSWORTH *shows hesitation.*]

ELLA. You'd prefer Dr. Chesher?

LADY B. No — I feel rather faint again.

   [*General consternation.*]

LADY B. [*Weeping copiously*]. And I have been so slighted. But sooner than make things unpleasant, I feel I'd better go home.

MARY [*Dropping* FELIX'S *arm, which she had taken*]. You take her in. [FELIX *demurs.*] Yes, do. It will please her. Lady Bodsworth, Mr. Galpin will take you in.

LADY B. Oh, no. It wouldn't be proper.

MARY. Oh, there's nothing improper —— [*Stops, remembering the word.*] I insist. Give her your arm, Felix.

[FELIX *offers his arm to* LADY BODSWORTH.]

LADY B. Oh, no, it would be a breach of etiquette.

MARY. Etiquette? This is just a little family dinner party. [*To* FELIX.] Take her in.

FELIX. Now, Lady Bodsworth ——

LADY B. No, please. I couldn't dream of going in before Lady Whichello — especially now she has been created ——

[*The thought causes a renewed fit of tears.*
FELIX *turns in despair to* ELLA.]

ELLA. Oh, take her, take her!

[TADMAN *manages to get to the table and takes a sly sip of his third cocktail.* FELIX *goes again to* LADY BODSWORTH *and offers arm.*]

LADY B. Oh, no — it's very kind — but I couldn't — no, really.

FELIX. Dear Lady Bodsworth, whom would you like to take you in?

LADY B. I'm sure I don't mind — don't think of me ——

MARY. What does it matter? We shan't get any dinner. I'll take you in! [*Taking* LADY BODS-WORTH'S *arm.*] Come along — Fanny!

> [*Taking her to door. The door is too narrow for them to go out together. They stand there, each of them making way for the other, and motioning each other to go first. MARY resolutely takes LADY BODSWORTH'S arm and drags her off.*]

CURTAIN.

NOTE

[The author is threatened with an action
for libel if he publishes this comedy without
revising it in form that will be acceptable
to Mr. George Whichelow of Bermondsey.
The author wishes to state that until the
production of the play he was unaware of
the existence of Mr. George Whichelow.
He regrets if he has inadvertently given any
annoyance to that gentleman, but is quite
unable to understand the reason for that
annoyance. It is obvious that if Mr. George
Whichelow's claim to revise this play is not
resisted, every author of a novel or a play
will in future be liable to a costly legal action from any person who happens to have
a similar name or trade to any one of the
characters in his work.]

It may be interesting to the American reader to
know that the action for libel was never brought
against Mr. Henry Arthur Jones, as it was found that
the plaintiff had no case.   — THE PUBLISHERS.

THE COUNTRY LIFE PRESS
GARDEN CITY, N. Y.